# INDEX

VIRAGO

*Patricia Williams*

**INDEX ON CENSORSHIP 2 1997**

Volume 26 No 2 March/April 1997 Issue 175

**Editor & Chief Executive**
Ursula Owen
**Deputy Editor**
Judith Vidal-Hall
**News Editor**
Adam Newey
**Production Editor**
Rose Bell
**Africa**
Adewale Maja-Pearce
**Eastern Europe**
Irena Maryniak
**Editorial Co-ordinator**
Nevine Mabro
**Fundraising Manager**
Elizabeth Twining
**Fundraising Assistant**
Joe Hipgrave
**Circulation & Marketing Director**
Louise Tyson
**Subscriptions & Promotions Manager**
Lotte Pang
**Office Manager**
Gary Netherton
**Website Manager**
Jules Nurrish
**Volunteer Assistants**
Jesse Banfield
Michaela Becker
Ann Chambers
Penny Dale
Nicholas McAulay
Cornelia Messing
Mansoor Mirza
Syra Morley
Philippa Nugent
Grazia Pelosi
Charles Peyton
Esther Scott
Nargess Shahmanesh
Sarah Smith
Briony Stocker
Emily Walmsley
Tara Warren

*Front cover:* © Bruno Barbey/ Magnum
*Back cover:* Patricia Williams © Virago

Cover design by Senate

**Directors** Louis Blom-Cooper, Ajay Chowdhury, Caroline Moorehead, Ursula Owen, Peter Palumbo, Jim Rose, Anthony Smith, Sue Woodford (Chair)

**Council** Ronald Dworkin, Amanda Foreman, Thomas Hammarberg, Clive Hollick, Geoffrey Hosking, Michael Ignatieff, Mark Littman, Pavel Litvinov, Robert McCrum, Uta Ruge, William Shawcross, Suriya Wickremasinghe

**Patrons** Chinua Achebe, David Astor, Robert L Bernstein, Harold Evans, Richard Hamilton, Stuart Hampshire, Yehudi Menuhin, Iris Murdoch, Philip Roth, Tom Stoppard, Michael Tippett, Morris West

**Australian committee** Phillip Adams, Blanche d'Alpuget, Bruce Dawe, Adele Horin, Angelo Loukakis, Ken Methold, Laurie Muller, Robert Pullan and David Williamson, c/o Ken Methold, PO Box 825, Glebe NSW 2037, Australia
**Danish committee** Paul Grosen, Niels Barfoed, Claus Sønderkøge, Herbert Pundik, Nils Thostrup, Toni Liversage and Björn Elmquist, c/o Claus Sønderkøge, Utkaervej 7, Ejerslev, DK-7900 Nykobing Mors, Denmark
**Dutch committee** Maarten Asscher, Gerlien van Dalen, Christel Jansen, Chris Keulemans, Wieke Rombach, Mineke Schipper and Steven de Winter, c/o Gerlien van Dalen and Chris Keulemans, De Balie, Kleine-Gartmanplantsoen 10, 1017 RR Amsterdam
**Norwegian committee** Trond Andreassen, Diis Bøhn, Helge Rønning and Sigmund Strømme, c/o Trond Andreassen, Tyrihansveren 8, N-0851 Oslo, Norway
**Swedish committee** Gunilla Abrandt and Ana L Valdés, c/o *Dagens Nyheter*, Kulturredaktionen, S-105 15 Stockholm, Sweden
**USA committee** Ariel Dorfman, Rea Hederman, Peter Jennings, Harvey J Kaye, Susan Kenny, Jane Kramer, Radha Kumar, Jeri Laber, Gara LaMarche, Anne Nelson, Faith Sale, Gaye Salisbury, Michael Scammell, Vivienne Walt

*Index on Censorship* (ISSN 0306-4220) is published bi-monthly by a non-profit-making company: Writers & Scholars International Ltd, Lancaster House, 33 Islington High Street, London N1 9LH *Tel:* 0171-278 2313  *Fax:* 0171-278 1878 *Email:* indexoncenso@gn.apc.org http://www.oneworld.org/index_oc/ *Index on Censorship* is associated with Writers & Scholars Educational Trust, registered charity number 325003
*Periodicals postage:* (US subscribers only) paid at Newark, New Jersey. Postmaster: send US address changes to *Index on Censorship* c/o Mercury Airfreight Int/ Ltd Inc, 2323 Randolph Avenue, Avenel, NJ 07001, USA

**Subscriptions 1997** (6 issues p.a.) Individuals: UK £38, US $50, rest of world £43 Institutions: UK £42, US $72, rest of world £48 Students: UK £25, US $35, rest of world £31

© This selection Writers & Scholars International Ltd, London 1997
© Contributors to this issue, except where otherwise indicated
Printed by Unwin Brothers Ltd, UK

*Index on Censorship* and Writers and Scholars Educational Trust depend on donations to guarantee their independence and to fund research The Trustees and Directors would like to thank all those whose donations support Index and WSET, including

Channel Four Television
Institusjonen Fritt Ord
The Norwegian Foreign Ministry
The Open Society Institute
The Rayne Foundation

Alan and Babette Sainsbury Charitable Trust
SIDA
UNESCO
United News and Media

**Former Editors:** Michael Scammell (1972-81); Hugh Lunghi (1981-83); George Theiner (1983-88); Sally Laird (1988-89); Andrew Graham-Yooll (1989-93)

# EDITORIAL

## Extremes of anxiety

The Convention on the Rights of the Child has broken all records as the most widely ratified human rights treaty in history (though the US has still not become party to it). Yet, on examining the state of the world's children, *Index* concludes there is less cause for congratulation than such commitment implies. The statistics, for a start, are surprising and disturbing. Child mortality rates may have fallen by 50 per cent since 1946, but an infant born in New York today is less likely to live to the age of five than one born in Shanghai. And though progress has been made on child malnutrition in developing countries, one in five American and one in three British children live below the poverty line.

It's a pretty violent world for children everywhere. Four thousand American children alone will be murdered by their parents this year, while Caroline Moorehead reports that more than 2 million children have been killed in wars over the past decade. In Sarajevo, one in four children were wounded: in Angola, seven out of 100 children have fired a gun at someone. Our Babel features Turkish children tortured in custody for the most minor of crimes — or none at all.

Forty million children live on the streets. Irena Maryniak laments their soaring numbers in Russia 'where democratisation has offered a vacuous universe with neither order nor rationale'. Closer to home, Marian Allsopp looks at images of victim and villain in the Jamie Bulger case, and growing anxiety about the role of family and state, while Edward Lucie-Smith observes our increasing self-consciousness over photographic images of children.

What sense can we make of the disparate childhoods described here? Only perhaps that children might reasonably conclude that confusion abounds among the grown-ups, no-one is much in control of their world, and not many people are even listening to them.

In our last issue before a crucial British election, Michael Foley looks at recent erosions of civil liberties, a frankly horrifying list — the treatment of asylum seekers, pregnant women, attempts to bug private telephones and the imposition of mandatory sentencing that would bypass the judiciary, to name but a few. E P Thompson, the great historian and passionate fighter for 'the freeborn Englishman', will be turning in his grave. ❑

# contents

# want
# the full
# story?

### Intolerance

The relaunch issue: Umberto Eco, Salman Rushdie, Dubravka Ugresic, Ronald Dworkin, Stephen Spender, James Fenton, Anne Nelson, Caroline Moorehead, Naguib Mahfouz, Vladimir Zhirinovsky, Alberto Manguel.

*(Index 1-2/1994)*

### Gay's the word

Gay life under Communism plus new work from Edmund White, Alberto Manguel, Emma Donoghue and Lionel Blue. Country file on Turkey with Yasar Kemal, Nicole Pope and Murat Belge. Report on independent radio in Africa.

*(Index 1/1995)*

### Liberty knell

Vaclav Havel on post-Communist life and Noam Chomsky on US foreign policy. Bob Sutcliffe and Isabelle Ligner on immigration. Nadine Gordimer and Jon Snow from South Africa.

*(Index 3/1994)*

*Provocative, subversive, eye-opening, opinion-shaping. Index constantly shows you the bugs underneath the blankets.*
—Index subscriber

### Liberty in Britain

Alan Clark, Andrew Puddephatt, Helena Kennedy and Gerry Adams look at threats to liberty in the UK. Mumia Abu-Jamal, Christopher Hitchens and Aryeh Neier on the resurgence of the death penalty in the USA. Alexander Solzhenitsyn on Chechnya.

*(Index 2/1995)*

### Media moguls

Ted Turner, Clive Hollick, Christopher Hird and Matthew Hoffman on concentration of media. Plus AS Byatt, Zoran Filipovic and Julian Barnes writing for Sarajevo.

*(Index 4-5/1994)*

### Rewriting history

Looks at the frenzy of revisionism as we approach the year 2000, with Ronald Dworkin, Felipe Fernandez-Armesto and Eduardo Galeano. South Africa file with Christopher Hope, Achmat Dangor and Nadine Gordimer.

*(Index 3/1995)*

### Post-wall world

The turbulent years since the Velvet Revolution: W L Webb, Ivan Klima and Ryszard Kapuscinski. Humanitarian aid as intervention: Alex de Waal in Africa, Jane Regan in Haiti, Julie Flint in Iraq.

*(Index 6/1994)*

### The body politic

A counter-agenda to the Beijing Conference for Women, with Erica Jong, Urvashi Butalia, Caroline Moorehead and Naila Kabeer. Plus Martha Gellhorn, Nestor Baguer and Ariel Hidalgo on Cuba.

*(Index 4/1995)*

## SAVE! Order the whole back issue collection and you save 15%

### UN: make or break

Michael Ignatieff, Tadeusz Mazowiecki, David Rieff and Alex de Waal on the problematic future of the UN. Liberty in the US by Anthony Lewis, Nadine Strossen, Patricia Williams and Andrei Codrescu.

*(Index 5/1995)*

### The subversive eye

Roman Polanski, John Waters, Kathryn Bigelow, Milos Forman, Arthur C Clarke, Quentin Tarantino, John Sayles, Ken Loach, Philip FrenchCosta Gavras and a host of others celebrate the extraordinary power and allure of 100 years of cinema.

*(Index 6/1995)*

*Intriguing blend of essays, photographs, and infographics, all of which remind us that human liberty and freedom of the press are inextricably linked.*
—Utne Reader

### Secret Chernobyls

Ten years on, the Chernobyl disaster is still growing. With Anthony Tucker, David Hearst and Mikhail Byckau. Plus the failure of human rights groups to communicate their message.

*(Index 1/1996)*

### Publishing now

Nadine Gordimer, Salman Rushdie, Alberto Manguel, Taslima Nasrin and Aryeh Neier on the threats, old and new, to publishing. Plus a survey of the critical press in the Middle East.

*(Index 2/1996)*

*Once again, I marvel when I see a copy of Index. The reason I marvel is that each of its yearly six issues manages to cram so much into 192 pages.*
—The Times

### US: Art unleashed

What kind of art is produced in the least censored country in the world? Roger Kimball, Edward Lucie-Smith and Judy Chicago respond.Plus John Lloyd, Vaclav Havel and Geoffrey Hosking look at Russia on the eve of critical elections.

*(Index 3/1996)*

### God is not dead

Darryl Pinckney, John Tusa, Baruch Kimmerling, John Simpson, Sami Zubaida and Abdolkarim Sorush examine the staggering resurgence of belief. Plus Saudi file with Alain Gresh, John Ware and Abdul Bari Atwan.

*(Index 4/1996)*

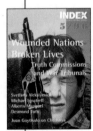

### Wounded nations

Michael Ignatieff, Desmond Tutu, Svetlana Aleksiyevich, Pieter-Dirk Uys , and Adam Michnik explore how countries come to terms with past horrors. Juan Goytisolo reports from Chechnya. Charles Glass on the US.

*(Index 5/1996)*

### Lost Words

Banned fiction from Ken Saro-Wiwa, Pramoedya Ananta Toer, Reinaldo Arenas, Bai Hua, Nedim Gursel and Ma Thida. Stories about silencing by Graham Greene, Ursula K Le Guin and Italo Calvino.

*(Index 6/1996)*

# get an INDEX !

## INDEX BACK ISSUES

- ❏ Intolerance (Index 1-2/1994)
- ❏ Liberty knell (Index 3/1994)
- ❏ Media moguls (Index 4-5/1994)
- ❏ Post-wall world (Index 6/1994)
- ❏ Gay's the word (Index 1/1995)
- ❏ Liberty in Britain (Index 2/1995)
- ❏ Rewriting history (Index 3/1995)
- ❏ The body politic (Index 4/1995)

- ❏ UN: make or break (Index 5/1995)
- ❏ The subversive eye (Index 6/1995)
- ❏ Chernobyl (Index 1/1996)
- ❏ Publishing now (Index 2/1996)
- ❏ US: Art unleashed (Index 3/1996)
- ❏ God is not dead (Index 4/1996)
- ❏ Wounded nations (Index 5/1996)
- ❏ Lost words (Index 6/1996)

**Single copy: £8**

**Discounts:**
Any four issues: **£30**
Any eight issues: **£58**
Any twelve issues: **£84**
All sixteen issues: **£108** *(you save £20)*

**SPECIAL OFFER**

**Postage:**
Outside the UK, please add £1 postage per issue ordered

Name

Address

**Payment:**
Payment by cheque, credit card, bank transfer or Giro

- ❏ I enclose a cheque (drawn on a UK bank) for £_____
- ❏ Charge my Visa/Mastercard/American Express

Card no

Expires          Signature

- ❏ I have instructed my bank to transfer £_____ to your bank account 0635788 at Lloyds Bank, 10 Hanover Square, London W1R 0BT
- ❏ I have sent £_____ to your Post Office National Giro account 574-5357 (Britain)

Please allow four to six weeks for delivery.

**RETURN TO:** INDEX, 33 Islington High Street, London N1 9LH
**Telephone**: (44) 0171-278-2313
**Facsimile**: (44) 171-278-1978
**E-mail**: indexoncenso@gn.apc.org
**Website** http://www.oneworld.org/index_oc/

www.oneworld.org

# MAKE CONTACT

The web is the perfect place to focus on issues neglected by the mainstream media: it's cheap, global, dynamic and almost entirely free of the usual vested interests. You can choose your audience and talk to them directly. If, that is, they know you're there. OneWorld is a community of over 100 websites devoted to human rights and sustainable development.

**Action:** campaigns, jobs, voluntary work and appeals from the whole community.

Click on **News** and you're in a daily news wire devoted entirely to global justice issues. It's updated daily, cross-indexed by date, country and theme and directly linked to the hottest news from every site on OneWorld.

It combines otherwise scattered websites into one authoritative source of infor-mation. OneWorld gets over 2 million hits a month from more than 100 countries, 60 of them in the South, and delivers 2 gigabytes of information every week.

**Anyone who publishes on the net quickly finds out that it's very easy to make a website. Shortly afterwards they discover that it's very difficult to make people come and look at it.**

The OneWorld supersite is the glue that holds all this together. It makes the community structured, searchable and accessible, with targeted sections designed to appeal to readers of different ages, interests and purposes. It's a library, a radio station, a discussion forum, a news wire and an art gallery, all gathered in one accessible place and all devoted to covering global justice issues.

**Blast** is a magazine for anyone who can't sit still. It links material from all over the site and gives it speed and attitude designed to appeal to younger readers.

The **Think Tank** and **Guides** offer professional debate and thematic pathways through the site. Readers following issues like landmines or women's rights can get the basics from a short, digestible guide then dig deeper, comparing views and responses from all sides.

When War Report became a OneWorld partner, their hits went up by 77% within a month. More hits mean more readers. OneWorld's huge audience is not the only benefit of partnership. Web space, training, site creation, fundraising, live databases, audio, video and much more are provided free or at charges far lower than the commercial rate.

It doesn't matter who makes your website or where it sits. All that matters is that people visit it. With OneWorld, they're on your doorstep.

OneWorld **Radio** is a global radio station delivered over the web and offered free to local community stations for rebroadcast ing.

# .faq

## Isn't the web just for rich countries?

OneWorld includes websites from the South free of charge, thanks to a grant from the European Union. If your NGO wishes to be one of our Southern Partners, please email debbie@oneworld.org or fax +44 1494 481 751.

## Is it just in English?

OneWorld Online carries material in several languages and plans to include many more, both southern and northern.

## Who funds OneWorld?

Only about 40% of our costs are met by partners' subscriptions and payments for services. Apart from our parent charity, the OneWorld Broadcasting Trust, we are also supported by the the European Union, British Telecom and the Overseas Development Administration.

## How much does it cost?

OneWorld partnership costs between £150 (US$225) and £600 (US$900) per year, depending on the size of your organisation.

OneWorld Online is wholly owned by the OneWorld Broadcasting Trust, charity number 296335. We are grateful to British Telecom for their support.

**news in the**

• **Send in the Mounties** An interesting case in Canada will, we hope, founder on the rock of that country's own confused statutes. While the age of consent in Canada is 14, the depiction of sexual activity between people under 18 is illegal. Two 16-year-old boys who taped themselves in the act and distributed said tape among friends have been arrested for 'distributing child pornography'. What now?

• **Further to the act** And in another odd little incident in Canada, the image it seems, even when fully clothed, is a dangerous thing. A man convicted of sex with a minor was found to have a magazine depicting young boys, all fully clothed. However, said the law, he was guilty — and sentenced him accordingly — of violating the child pornography laws because to him 'these images were stimulating'.

• **Democratic exhaustion** Pakistan's recent election was a bit of an anticlimax. One discredited party replaced another; the international cricketer Imran Khan failed to get a single seat and the main religious party, the Jamiat e Islami, did not stand. But the greatest defeat was for democracy: the turnout was little more than 30 per cent.

• **Holy season** The escalation of killings that accompanies Islam's fasting month of Ramadan in Algeria each year is notorious though never adequately explained. This year, over 300 civilians, sometimes whole families, lost their lives. The orgy of assassinations that ushered in the feast at the end of the fast topped all records: 28 people, including a baby, were massacred in honour of Eid al Fitr.

• **White as the Alpine snow** The Swiss have announced the creation of a fund of US$70 million for 'needy victims of the

Holocaust'. Too little, too late, and no way to launder a sorry history. What about all those 'disappeared' documents recording Swiss collaboration with Nazi companies throughout World War II?

• **Afghanistan's Taliban** have tightened their grip on Kabul. Men have nine days to sprout a healthy Islamic beard; not only must women sport the all-enveloping Afghan version of the *chador* and stay away from work, they may not keep the company of strangers. Two French aid workers were arrested at the end of February for violating Islamic law by attending a lunch given by local female workers for Action contre la faim (Action against hunger).

• **Sixty-five million Americans**, one-third of an average Sunday night audience, watched Steven Spielberg's *Schindler's List* on prime-time TV on 23 February. It was twice as many who saw it in the cinema and confounded programmers who had predicted a disaster. Republican congressman Tom Coburn protested against the 'violence and nudity' in the film but was persuaded to beat a hasty retreat by fellow Republican Al d'Amato.

• **Africa's forgotten war** in the Western Sahara has reached 'total deadlock' after 21 years, according to Polisario Front leader M Salem ould Salek. The UN team having failed to organise the referendum that would, in theory, liberate the Western Sahara from Moroccan control, may withdraw shortly, leaving Polisario to resort once more to war against Morocco.

• **Burma's longest-running rebellion** looks as though it has run out of steam. Since mid-February, 16,000 Karen refugees have fled from the Burmese military to join the 60,000 members of their tribe already across the border in Thailand. The Karen lands are the site of important industrial development projects: a deep-water port, railway and the gas pipeline being constructed by Total. Many Karens have been pressed into forced labour on these projects.

• **Tamil tribulations** All available evidence from witnesses inside Sri Lanka points to a renewed military onslaught on the island's Tamils. Priests working within the community in Jaffna report a renewed campaign since the end of last year. The chief executive of the British Refugee Council, Nick Hardwick, who visited Sri Lanka in December, says, 'I met and talked to people who bore the visible scars of the torture they'd received at the hands of military. Serious human rights violations are clearly continuing.'

• **Meanwhile, back in Britain**, Mr Hardwick's report is unlikely to melt the heart of the UK Home Office that continues to return Sri Lankan asylum seekers to Colombo, regardless of the 'grave concern for their safety' expressed by the Refugee Council and others. Up to 1993, over 97 per cent of asylum seekers were allowed to stay in the UK. Since then, 95 per cent have been refused despite the deteriorating situation.

• **Jean-Marie Le Pen**'s xenophobic National Front Party moves from strength to strength among the French electorate. Despite his anti-immigration platform, the latest government figures show that immigration into France has not increased over the last 20 years. Nor do immigrants rob the French of jobs: they make up the majority of France's 12 per cent unemployed (see below).

• **The tanks were out** in force in Ankara this February when Turkey's army took exception to what it claimed was a threat to the secular state. The Refah — Turkey's ruling Welfare Party — mayor of a poverty-stricken suburb of the capital had made the mistake of welcoming in Eid with a public declaration of his preference for a more Islamic style of government. The mayor went to gaol; the army, self-appointed guardians of Ataturk's secular state, is getting restless under the present government's Islamic inclinations.

• **'The trouble with books is they make people intolerant'** comments philosophy professor Fernando Savater in the Spanish daily, *El País*, only partly in jest. Bookshops have been front-page news in Spain of late following the official closure of one and repeated vandalism of another. The first, Europa, specialised in pro-Nazi and racist literature; the second was the victim of ETA enthusiasts in San Sebastian anxious to impose their diktat throughout their Basque homeland. As the professor points out, admonishing the offending parties to 'err on the side of liberty rather than repression', neither attack has much to do with books, more with the free expression of opinion in a plural society. He does, however, take comfort in the fact that, contrary to popular mythology, the book is evidently not an endangered species.

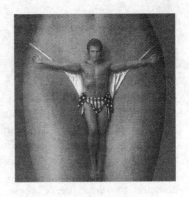

• **Banned in the USA** for 'insulting the flag'; withdrawn by its director in France after being accused of being 'offensive to religion'; a potential victim of Britain's archaic blasphemy laws when it arrives in the UK at the end of March. The distributors of Milos Forman's latest film, *The People vs Larry Flynt*, just couldn't get it together with their publicity poster. If the film, already nominated for two Oscars, is half as irreverent as the poster it will do well.

• **No win** Japan's Kanagawa Human Rights Centre (KHRC) ran into trouble when it criticised local politicians' statements on Korean comfort women and the Japanese colonisation of Korea. Alarmed by assertions that the comfort women were not forced into slavery and that Korea was 'improved' by the experience of colonisation by a 'higher quality of people', KHRC protested against the invitation of one such speaker to address a local business community meeting and promptly found itself accused of 'oppressing freedom of speech' in *Yomiuri-Shinbun*, Japan's largest national paper. Since the article appeared (on 31 January) KHRC has been inundated with protests from angry nationalists supporting the offending opinion, and worried liberals supporting the right to free expression.

• **Combat fatigue...** 'Conflict is a form of communication. Although it is possible to communicate without conflict, conflict without some type of communication is impossible,' say Abiodun Onadipe and David Lord in *African Conflict and the Media,* the latest publication from Conciliation Resources (UK). They offer a timely reminder that the media whose freedom we defend so hotly is not always on the side of the angels. In Rwanda and the former Yugoslavia it was instrumental in inciting whole populations to war and genocide; in neither of those places, let alone in any other of Africa's conflict zones — like Zaire, for instance — has it made much effort to communicate the underlying causes of conflict, provide a forum for public debate that might aid reconciliation or offered 'constructive alternatives to violence and despair'. A need, they conclude, that is 'more urgent, and the obstacles that much greater, in African societies wracked by widespread social violence or civil war'. ❏

## HARVEY J KAYE

# US notebook

• **China — handle with care** In spite of the Chinese government's continuing record of massive human rights abuses, Bill Clinton recently welcomed to the White House General Chi Haotian, the officer who commanded the Chinese army's June 1989 murderous assault on demonstrators in Tiananmen Square. At the same time, the conservative American magazine, the *Weekly Standard*, reports that 'a Massachusetts company, Bay Networks, is investing in technology designed to allow [the Chinese government] to censor the Internet, whose Chinese users must already register with the police.'

• **Can you keep a secret?** A federal judge in the US District Court in San Francisco ruled in favour of University of Illinois mathematics professor Daniel Bernstein's suit claiming that elements of the Arms Export Control Act violated the First Amendment. In her decision, Judge Marilyn Hall Patel declared unconstitutional certain government controls and prohibitions on the export of computer encryption programmes. According to the *Chronicle of Higher Education*, Professor Bernstein argued that the government's rules violated his right of free speech for it meant he would have had to 'register as an arms dealer and seek government permission before publishing his work'.

• **Annie get your gun** In October 1996, Idaho superintendent of public instruction Anne Fox announced that school districts 'would not be eligible for federal AIDS education dollars unless they offered abstinence-based sex education programmes'. In further pursuit of her conservative political agenda — and believing it a perfect varsity pastime for the students of this pro-gun, pro-hunting state — Fox recently proposed that 'shooting sports' become an extracurricular activity in Idaho's junior and senior high schools. In the face of rising school violence, and worried about liability and safety, the Idaho High School Activities Association turned down the proposal.

• **RSVP** The National Advertising Review Council, the marketing industry's self-regulatory organisation, has announced that it will not create industry-wide, age-specific guidelines for commercials. In the wake of the liquor industry's termination of its self-imposed ban on television and radio advertising of distilled spirits; the more favourable public reception of the American broadcast networks' creation of a ratings system indicating the appropriate viewing age of a particular television programme; *and* the promulgation of federal regulations restricting tobacco ads directed at minors, it's assumed that the Council's failure to come up with its own guidelines invites government regulation.

• **The Rockford files** The school board in Rockford, Illinois, has banned from school libraries the Curbstone Press book *Always Running: La Vida Loca — Gang Days in LA* by former gang member Luis Rodriguez. In the book Rodriguez explains his motivation to join and then escape gang life and he calls for a 'reorganisation of American society' as an alternative to the prevailing urban tragedy. One board member called the work 'harmful, ungodly and wrong...irreligious, anti-family, left-wing, anti-American, and radical'; another remarked that 'to really do some good, the book should be kept from the public altogether' because reading it makes 'you think about sex and drugs'.

• **Why Johnny can't read 1** Decrying its educational and cultural implications, columnists and public figures across the country were incensed by the school board's decision in Oakland, California, to recognise African-American 'ghetto' speech — known as Ebonics — as a language separate from English. Overwhelmed by the hostile response, the board rescinded its decision.

• **Why Johnny can't read 2** Pundits and politicians accorded far less attention to a Fairness and Accuracy in Reporting (FAIR) report on the for-profit television news and advertising programme Channel One, which is broadcast daily to eight million public school students around the nation. Mark Crispin Miller, Johns Hopkins University media studies professor and co-author of *How to be Stupid: The Teachings of Channel One*, writes 'its real function is not journalistic but commercial.'

• **We've just begun to fight** Promoters of the 1996 Telecommunications Act promised that the Act would increase competition, assure a diversity of media voices and thus benefit Americans as citizens and consumers. One year on, the only certainty is that the Act engendered a wave of media mergers, including that of Time Warner and Turner to create the world's largest media company. Nevertheless, progressive media activists, critics and scholars have not given up the fight for a 'democratic media' controlled by the people and for the people rather than the corporations. A vast coalition of progressive groups, co-ordinated by the Learning Alliance, convened the 'Freeing the Media' conference (31 January-1 February) in New York City. ❏

*Harvey J Kaye is professor of social change and development at the University of Wisconsin-Green Bay and the author of* Why Do Ruling Classes Fear History? and Other Questions *(1996)*

• **'Dear Mr President,** I am called Judith Lorant. I am nine years old and go to the Sully school in Nantes. I know you are the greatest president of all and that's why I'm writing to ask you to stop all these bad men. They want to prevent me having my Grandmother Aïsha and my Aunt Mana to stay with me on my birthday.

'It's not fair you know: my mother is really sad because as well as being Berber, she is also French.

'I want to invite my grandmother and Mana to my birthday just like my friends. You know, my cousin Laetitia, Uncle Abdou's daughter, is just as sad as me not to be able to see our Granny. Granny and Mana are not a danger to France. I swear it! And anyway, my home is Granny's home too. When I go to Morocco, her house is my house. Please, Mr Chirac, stop these awful men from closing the door on these people. I can't wait to get your reply. And I give you a great big hug.'

Judith's letter was published in Morocco's *Libération*, in response to France's Loi Debré, now going through Parliament. The law requires that all foreign visitors without residence permits be reported by their hosts to the authorities. In the absence of a lead from any of France's opposition parties, artists and intellectuals took the initiative in protesting the law.

• **In the name of the law** Set aside for a moment the question of whether the laws of the Islamic Republic of Iran are good laws or bad laws. Consider instead that about 60 million Iranians have to wake up every morning and go about their daily lives there. Questions of more immediate interest to them might be: What is the law? Can I keep out of trouble by obeying it? The answer to the first question seems to be increasingly irrelevant since the answer to the second question is an emphatic 'no'.

When a bookshop was attacked in Tehran in August 1995, the 'offending' book (*And the Gods Laugh on Mondays*) — published legally with the permission of the Ministry of Islamic Guidance — was banned and no known attempt was made to bring the arsonists to justice. When, in May 1996, a group of people beat up spectators and broke the windows at a cinema showing the film *Gift from India* — licensed by the same Ministry — no light was shed on the fate of the attackers, but the film was withdrawn from the public eye. When a university lecturer (Abdolkarim Sorush) was harassed, his wife and family threatened, and his lectures disrupted every time he arrived at Tehran University to teach his course in the philosophy of the social sciences, he seemed to have no recourse to the law. His contract was not renewed and nothing more was heard about the aggressors. (Not surprisingly, letters from zealous students asking for this or that lecturer to be removed from their post have become a regular feature of the Iranian press.)

When programmes are broadcast on Iranian media and articles published in newspapers describing writers, lecturers and artists as 'fifth-columnists', 'mercenaries' and 'traitors', no official seems to feel any need to explain why, if these charges are true, the relevant people have not been put on trial; or why, if the charges are unfounded, they can be slandered with such impunity using public funds?

Most worrying of all, Faraj Sarkoohi, editor of the literary journal *Adineh* published in Tehran, who disappeared on 3 November last year, reappeared at Tehran's Mehrabad airport on 20 December and disappeared again on 26 January. An extremely disturbing letter, written by Sarkoohi, suggests that he has been subjected to extreme physical and mental duress by people purporting to be employees of the Iranian Intelligence Ministry (see page 90). An official Iranian report on 4 February said that Sarkoohi and his brother, Esma'il, had been arrested on 3 February while trying to flee the country through the southern port of Bushehr. The report said they had promised to pay two smugglers 20 million rials (US$4,750) to help them leave the country.

In the light of Article 32 of the Iranian Constitution that states: 'No-one may be arrested except with the procedure laid down by the law. In case of arrest, charges, with the reasons for the accusation, must, without delay, be communicated and explained to the accused in writing, and a provisional dossier must be forwarded to the competent judicial authorities within a maximum of 24 hours,' and Article 37 that presumes innocence; and Article 38 that outlaws torture, can any Iranian official explain what is happening to Faraj Sarkoohi and why? In the name of the law. *Nilou Mobasser*

• **Hold the front page** Throughout the siege of the Japanese ambassador's residence in Peru, the Tupac Amaru Revolutionary Movement (MRTA) have been one step ahead of the government in understanding what makes the media tick and in the exploitation of hi-tech. While President Fujimori tries to convince the international community that it's business as usual, the rebels have captured the imagination of the world.

Similarities with the Zapatistas in Mexico are obvious. The leader of the MRTA, Néstor Cerpa, like Subcomandante Marcos, has used modern communications to promote his image and his cause. He is the romantic hero; his group the voice of the impoverished and marginalised. 'Che he's not,' says one impressed hostage. 'But he's definitely got something.'

The storming of the Japanese embassy was directed using a cellular phone; in a live radio interview with Radio Programmas del Peru, Cerpa stated the group's demands for the release of the hostages; a press conference inside the besieged embassy allowed him to condemn Fujimori's political and economic policies before the world's media; and 'Rebel Voice', the group's Internet site, ensures the world is regularly updated with the MRTA's communiqués.

All too aware of the rebels' media success, the Peruvian government has repeatedly tried to control their access to any form of communication. Its attempts have proved fruitless. Disruption of cellular and wire-line telephone services only drove the rebels back to basics: they placed messages to journalists in the windows and on the roof of the embassy.

Efforts to prevent the media from actively seeking out the rebels have been just as problematic. Two Japanese journalists from TV Asahi managed to break into the residency and conduct an interview with Cerpa. They were later arrested and their tape confiscated by the Peruvian authorities. On New Year's Eve, the rebels stepped outside the compound to address the press. While filming was taking place, several journalists breached security and dashed into the building. The result was an impromptu press conference in which interviews with both the rebels and the hostages were transmitted live.

Seventy-four hostages are still being held and, weeks into the siege,

scores of journalists wait outside the embassy to see how it will end. However it goes, Cerpa is assured of the front page. *Nevine Mabro*

• **Prisoner without a conscience**
The eagerness of Amnesty International and Reporters Sans Frontières to uphold the principle of freedom of expression — even when it was not an issue — sent them rushing into an international campaign in support of a man whose behaviour during the Rwandan genocide has been corroborated by 34 witnesses.

In their report *Witness to Genocide*, published at the end of January, African Rights document the case of Joseph Ruyenzi, a former teacher turned newsreader with Radio Rwanda, currently imprisoned in Kigali accused of the rape and sexual mutilation of Donatilla Mujawimana (*Index* 3/1996, 4/1996).

Within two days of his arrest on 30 March last year, Ruyenzi's case was taken up by Amnesty and RSF as evidence of 'a pattern of government victimisation of journalists in Rwanda' and 'ethnic purification' of the state-run media. Ruyenzi himself, however, never claimed that his position at the radio station was what led to his arrest.

African Rights' eight-month investigation into allegations against Ruyenzi has wider implications. 'By supporting Ruyenzi, they [AI and RSF] are hardening the disillusion of survivors; belittling the experiences of all victims of rape during the genocide in Rwanda and undermining their quest for justice,' say African Rights.

Amnesty has since dropped Ruyenzi from its urgent action list and RSF now admits the case is not as straightforward as previously assumed. Donatilla Mujawimana, meanwhile, has been vilified in the local press while Ruyenzi has been cast as the victim. *Penny Dale*

---

## Andrei Donatovich Sinyavsky, 8 October 1925 - 25 February 1997

SUE ADLER/THE OBSERVER

ANDREI SINYAVSKY is dead. We mourn him at *Index* not only as one of the greatest writers of twentieth-century Russia and a lifelong opponent of censorship, but in a more intimate way. It was as the result of a letter to *The Times* appealing for international support for two dissident writers, then on trial in Moscow for 'anti-Soviet activities', that *Index* was born 25 years ago. The writers were Andrei Sinyavsky and Yuli Daniel; the trial, as Michael Scammell, first editor of the magazine, writes in his *Guardian* obituary, 'was a landmark in Soviet political history. It was the first time since the 1920s that individuals had been openly tried for their opinions, and also the first time that defendants in a show trial had defied their judges and prosecutors.'

Sinyavsky was sentenced to seven years' hard labour. On his release five and a half years later, he emigrated to Paris where he died on 25 February. *A Voice from the Chorus*, written during his imprisonment and published in 1973, is one of the first and most revealing books to have come out of the labour camps. The magazine he founded in Paris with his wife Maria Rozanova in 1978 still continues. Unlike so many of its emigre counterparts, *Sintaksis* remained as independent of western propaganda and the more rabid politics of exile as it was hostile to Soviet coercion.

It is comforting to know that until his own death in 1989, Daniel, who remained in Russia, kept him regularly supplied with his favourite brand of *papirossi* — 'Bielamorkanal'. ❑

# INDEX

# THE CRUCIBLE

SALMAN RUSHDIE braved the rain and the *fatwa* to support *Index* and Writers & Scholars Educational Trust at the Gala Première of the film of Arthur Miller's play *The Crucible,* starring Daniel Day-Lewis, Winona Ryder and Paul Scofield. Those who regularly attend *Index* events will know that heavy rain is a common feature. But it did not dampen everyone's enjoyment of a fine and powerful film about truth on trial.

*Index on Censorship* was founded in response to show trials from another period — of writers in the Soviet Union, one of whom, Andrei Sinyavsky, has just died (see page 15). Twenty-five years later, the Communist world gone, censorship is still with us, and intolerance has appeared in some powerful new guises — religious fanaticism and ethnic cleansing being two of them. The need for *Index* is as strong as ever.

The film has significance for our current work and for our history. Arthur Miller is a long-time supporter of *Index*, while Paul

EastEnders *star Pam St Clement arriving at the prem*ière

GEORGE BODNER

Scofield, and Daniel Day-Lewis's father, Cecil Day-Lewis, both signed the telegram of protest to the Soviet authorities that was the birth of *Index*. So the première of *The Crucible* was the ideal event to launch our 25th-anniversary year.

*Index* would like to thank all those who made this occasion possible: Twentieth Century Fox, Odeon Cinemas, all our sponsors, and our première committee, especially its chairman Amanda Foreman.

# MICHAEL FOLEY

# Swinging by a thread

**London is the swinging capital of the world once more, say the media. But there is another, darker side to Britain in the 1990s where the dying days of its government are characterised by defensiveness, meanness of spirit and lack of compassion**

BRITAIN is chic and US magazines fill their feature pages with its resurgence as a centre of fashion and culture. We hear much less about the harsh treatment meted out to refugees and those escaping repressive regimes; of plans for harsh and illiberal laws that run contrary to civil liberties; of a justice system that accepts there are many more Bridgewater Threes wrongfully imprisoned. Journalists comment almost casually that Britain's jails hold many innocent people, and no-one seems at all surprised.

The incarceration of Roisin McAliskey raises similar concerns. She is in an advanced state of pregnancy and, because she is wanted by a foreign government, is being held as a high security prisoner and will, it was reported, be handcuffed while she gives birth. She has been found guilty of nothing. Though later denied, the rumour was all too believable in the present climate and gained widespread credence. And there could be worse to come: the authorities may remove the child from its mother at birth.

There are too many indications that the British establishment is intent on eroding civil liberties. The Jurisdiction (Conspiracy and Incitement) Bill came within a whisper of being passed by the House of Commons; the government views its present defeat as no more than a temporary set-back that it will hasten to rectify. Now that the Ulster Unionists have agreed to continue propping up John Major's administration for whatever they can get out of it, loss of an overall majority is unlikely to affect this or any other repressive legislation.

Yet the Conspiracy Bill, would, and may still, undermine something Britain has been justifiably proud of: the sanctuary it afforded political dissidents. In the mid-nineteenth century, the Prussian government tried to persuade the British government that Karl Marx should be transported to the Colonies. That did not happen, of course, and Marx spent many years availing himself of that great British institution, the British Library.

The Conspiracy Bill is an attack on political exiles. If it does ever become law, it will become, for the first time in British history, a criminal act to incite or conspire in activities against a foreign country from exile in Britain. According to Seumas Milne and Richard Norton-Taylor, writing in the *Guardian*, though a Private Member's Bill, this particular bit of chicanery was 'cooked up by the government to pacify foreign governments — notably Saudi Arabia — in the wake of last year's botched attempts to expel the Saudi dissident Mohammed al Mas'ari...the measure was one of a series of sops offered to King Fahd by the foreign secretary, Malcolm Rifkind, during his fence-mending visit to Riyadh last summer.'

But what they found extraordinary, say Milne and Norton-Taylor, was that such a sweeping change in UK law, one that would have a far reaching impact on the rights of British nationals as well as political refugees, could have been rushed through the Commons with the broad support of the main opposition parties and with barely a whisper of media comment.

While the Home Office minister claimed it was aimed at paedophiles and football hooligans, other official sources indicated its main target was those who support political violence against foreign governments, a category that would, in its day, have included Nelson Mandela, hundreds of Chilean exiles opposed to the Pinochet regime, opponents of the Pol Pot regime in Democratic Kampuchea, not to mention those who continue to oppose Indonesia's occupation of East Timor.

The Bill reflects Britain's uncertainty in the world today. Before the end of the Cold War, the political exile was welcome in Britain. They tended to be enemies of Britain's Communist enemies, intellectuals organising opposition to the regimes of Eastern and central Europe.

Today the issues are not so clear-cut. When Saddam Hussein was being backed by the West, opposition groups could have run foul of such a law;

*Rochester gaol, February 1997: mass picket protests immigration laws on the 34th day of the hunger strike Credit: Stalingrad O'Neill*

today, of course, they would not. Right of sanctuary would be replaced by political expediency and Britain free to appease any government it felt a need to cosy up to — regardless of its human rights record.

MEANWHILE, another event to which the media paid remarkably little attention until it reached crisis point, is the continuing hunger strike of asylum seekers held in Rochester prison. Many have been in gaol awaiting a hearing for several years without having committed any crime. They come from Algeria, Nigeria, Romania, Zaire... They are denied even that most fundamental of British rights, habeas corpus.

The British government continues to rail against the 'flood' of bogus asylum seekers as though this were, in itself, an adequate reason for depriving people of the most basic rights of any decent society. Some may indeed have absolutely no right to be in Britain; others, for all we know, may be escaping justice back home. None of this should override their right to a hearing before a judge in a British court; but then asylum seekers should be bearded intellectuals accused of distributing *samizdat* material, not peasants fearing for their lives, nor secular North Africans afraid of Muslim fundamentalists.

Meanwhile, the Labour Party is poised on the cusp of power and has become more cautious. Tony Blair's spokesman, Alastair Campbell, said in an interview recently that the two most influential newspapers in the UK are the *Daily Mail* and the *Sun*. Fears of being found 'too soft on crime' in the media generally, but particularly in those two newspapers, means that Labour has supplied no real nor effective opposition to two specific pieces of legislation directly threatening civil liberties. The first proposed to give the police wide bugging powers; the second to bypass the judiciary by imposing mandatory minimum sentencing for persistent offenders, notably burglars and drug dealers.

Some might ask what is new in all this. Irish people, in particular, might view sudden concern about civil liberties with a raised eyebrow. The Prevention of Terrorism Act, the infamous PTA, rushed through by a Labour government, has been on the statute books for over 25 years. As a piece of legislation it never achieved its stated purpose: to increase the police's scope in combating terrorism. What it did allow was trawling trips by the police through Irish communities in Britain, and the harassment of Irish people travelling between Ireland and Britain. But there was a feeling that the PTA might have been an exception; that it reflected a particular problem — Britain's 'Irish problem' in the North. We probably missed something back in the 1970s: the PTA was only the beginning of the downward slide.

It is as if the new world order, so heartily welcomed by Margaret Thatcher, has proved too complex to handle. Britain today seems comfortable neither with the globalisation so warmly embraced by the Tories, nor the cosmopolitanism that was always one of the country's great attractions. Globalisation is good when it is about capital, not so appealing when it confronts us with the culture, politics and ideas of those at the other end of the global market. Those people locked up in Rochester prison are part of that same globalisation; the Conspiracy Bill

● ● ● ● ● ● ● ● ● ● ● ● ● ● ● ● ● ● ● ● ● ● ● ● ● ● ● ● ● ● ● ● ● ● ● ●

**Globalisation, so warmly embraced by the Tories, is good when it is about capitalism, not so appealing when it confronts us with the culture, politics and ideas of those at the other end of the global market**

● ● ● ● ● ● ● ● ● ● ● ● ● ● ● ● ● ● ● ● ● ● ● ● ● ● ● ● ● ● ● ● ● ● ● ●

would seem to be the only response of which the government is capable.

The British press conference at the summit concluding the Irish presidency of the European Union (EU) in December said it all: it was a dispiriting affair. Here was an important meeting of 15 heads of government, discussions had been wide-ranging and important. Yet, when it came to the UK press conference, the British press corps were interested only with internal domestic trivia. What were the differences between John Major and his Chancellor? What about the support of the Spice Girls for Margaret Thatcher as reported by the *Spectator*. The correspondents of Europe's media, who had travelled to Dublin for the occasion, were bemused.

Britain's problems reflect an increasingly inward-looking country. It is not the only EU member that has problems with the direction Europe is taking. Sweden, now a reluctant member, responds by seeking a Union more committed to openness and transparency. Britain fears the changes taking place around it and takes refuge in Euro-isolationism.

Nor, despite its move toward greater transparency in government, is

Britain much less obsessed with its old habits of secrecy. Ireland, possibly even more secret than Britain, will have its Freedom of Information Act this year and looks set to repeal its Official Secrets Act. Labour has promised Freedom of Information legislation, a move in the right direction.

However, there are worrying signs that others in the EU are coming to accept Britain's stance on certain issues. The European Court of Human Rights, whose record on free expression is honourable and which castigated Britain more often than any other member of the EU, has recently ruled in favour of Britain's archaic blasphemy laws in a judgement that unexpectedly upheld the UK banning of the *Visions of Ecstasy* video (*Index* 1/1997). One can only hope that UK threats to ignore the jurisdiction of the European Court of Human Rights will not put it under pressure to bow to the British view of things. ❏

*Michael Foley* is media correspondent at the Irish Times

## NEED A NEWS FIX?

Keep up with the latest stories by checking out our website and APC conference. Every two weeks INDEX publishes censorship news from around the world. Along with updates from our editorial team, you'll find news by journalists who are banned in their own country.

**INDEX**online

http://www.oneworld.org/index___oc/
apc conference: index.censor

## POLLY BIDE

# Mean streets

**Following in the dubious footsteps of New York, London
proposes to go even further with its 'license to film'.
Infringement will be a criminal offence**

IT'S three o'clock in the afternoon on a quiet street. A cameraman is
setting up his tripod to take a shot of a house where he has just filmed
an interview. When the producer joins him outside, a policeman appears
and demands their film permit. The producer says she had no time to
contact the local licensing office. But the policeman isn't interested. The
producer has committed a criminal offence.

Where is this happening? Surely not in London? Licensing systems
such as this normally exist only under the most despotic regimes. But
now an extraordinary piece of legislation threatens the freedom to film on
the streets of our own capital. Tucked away among the other diverse
proposals of the Seventh London Local Authorities Bill, is, in essence, a
system of film licences for all programme-makers filming on the public
highway or public open spaces. This is a Private Bill promoted by the
London borough councils and the City of London, not by an MP.

The Bill will have its second reading in the House of Lords on 12
March. If the relevant clauses become law, any failure by a producer to
give reasonable written notice of filming will be a criminal offence. Local
councils will be authorised to charge for the assistance they give. The only
crews who will be exempt from this licensing will be news crews shooting
material for transmission that day or the following day. And yet, those
who drafted this Bill have the temerity to suggest that these new
regulations are designed to 'give assistance' to the film industry in
London.

It would be easier to understand the motivation for this Bill if there
were a huge problem that needed to be addressed by universal licensing.

But there is no evidence of any widespread difficulty. Perhaps the idea was born from the notion that such a scheme would produce a financial windfall for the London boroughs. Instead, it seems completely possible that such a law will drive some programme-makers — and the considerable benefits they bring — out of the metropolis altogether. Documentary production, part of the public service remit of both the BBC and Channel 4, would be particularly affected.

The Bill was partly inspired by a request from the London Film Commission who wanted the powers of borough councils to close roads, on behalf of film producers, put on a statutory basis. However useful this may be, it seems as if the Bill's promoters believe that all productions involve the same degree of nuisance and disruption as a feature film or period drama. The Bill fails to recognise that, in these days of small crews and even tighter budgets, most factual productions cause little or no obstruction or annoyance to the public at all.

Much of the time, when filming on the street, I work with just two or three other people. Our equipment is easily carried and rarely involves either cabling or lighting. As digital technology progresses, even the cameras we use are shrinking. Soon it may be hard to distinguish us from amateur video enthusiasts. But, as a professional, I would be penalised by this new law — and so, in my case, would the licence-payer. I would have to pay for the right to film at whatever rate the local authority sees fit to charge me. Such payments would particularly penalise low-budget productions and present yet another challenge to the quality of such programmes.

We are in a public place; we try to limit disturbance to the public; and there is no trespass. Rather than helping us, the proposed legislation attacks our current working practices, especially during observational filming where a quick response is essential. More seriously, the Bill represents a direct assault on valued freedoms within our democracy — of which the ability to inform our audience about events which occur in public places is surely one. Will stills photographers or radio and newspaper journalists also be required to apply for permission to work? The fact that such a suggestion can even be voiced indicates just how all-embracing these proposals are.

Producers are usually conscious of situations where they may require additional help from local authorities or, more commonly, from the police. In such circumstances, we have always been willing to pay for any assistance given, within reasonable limits. But a blanket permit scheme would be totally excessive and, what is more, impossible to enforce. Will we really have to seek permission every time we place a tripod at the edge of a road for five minutes? When filming actuality, will we have to stop filming when our subject suddenly decides to take an unplanned walk down the street — or risk appearing in front of a magistrate to defend our decision to follow him?

Anyone who has filmed in Manhattan knows how unenforceable their permit system is. Set up with the intention of encouraging film production in the city, free permits allow you to film at specific road junctions at prearranged times. Essentially the system ensures that the producer indemnifies the city authorities for any personal injury or damage to property incurred during filming. Except for major feature film productions, everyone is constantly in breach of their permit — whether delayed by city traffic or capturing an unplanned shot. However, in New York there is a crucial difference. The film crew without a valid permit is not committing a crime. The worst the producer faces would be a fine for a minor civil offence. In fact, this hardly ever happens.

Neither I nor my colleagues either inside or outside the BBC see any benefit whatsoever in these proposals. The idea that any infringement of these regulations would lead to criminal charges is particularly offensive. What is more, the legislation would impose severe limitations on filming for both practical and financial reasons — and so restrict legitimate and sometimes democratically desirable business. Imagine trying to acquire a permit to film the exterior of a town hall from a local authority whose officials are accused of fraud or corruption.

The relevant section of the Bill has been drafted without reference either to producers or to the major broadcasters. Most people in the industry have not even heard of it yet. But petitions against the Bill have now been deposited in the House of Lords from the BBC, Channel 4 and Carlton Television. Now factual programme-makers can only hope that, following discussion, this ill-conceived proposal will be as swiftly dismissed as it deserves. ❏

*Polly Bide is a documentary producer and director, currently working with the BBC in London*

# INTERVIEW

## NICOLA LACEY

# Talking about race quietly

**Patricia J Williams, American law professor and this year's BBC Reith lecturer, returns race to the centre of everyday discourse — and meets the media en route**

VIRAGO

IN the European Year against Racism, an American law professor came to Britain with the modest ambition of contributing to a civilised public conversation about 'the persistence of prejudice'. Since she came from one of the top US law schools, equipped with a considerable reputation as both writer and broadcaster, and in response to an invitation to speak from one of the most prestigious platforms in the world — the BBC's Reith Lectures — she might reasonably have disembarked from the plane in a cautiously optimistic frame of mind. Her optimism, however, was to be short-lived. Within a matter of days — and before a single word of her lectures had been broadcast — a storm of invective from those unable or unwilling to listen to her arguments sought to transform quiet talk into silence, and civilised discourse disintegrated into the cacophony of closed minds.

The professor might well have comforted herself with the thought that this noise was eloquent, if ugly, testimony to the veracity of some of her central claims — notably her claim that contemporary social discourse is marked by a denial of the relevance of race, in a movement of repression which engenders hysterical reactions to attempts to make race visible. She might also have found solace in the thought that the press reaction underlined the importance of her commitment to asking whether a different sort of conversation about race could be engendered. There was, however, little to console those 'people of good will' whom she sought to address, and they were left to reflect upon the distance yet to be travelled towards the state of 'grace' evoked in the title of the professor's lectures: *A Genealogy of Race: Towards a Theory of Grace*.

Meeting Patricia Williams, one is immediately aware that she is too wise to have been as optimistic as the professor in my story. She is also too gracious to have taken comfort from the way in which the reaction to her presence in some sections of the press confirms her own hypotheses. Elegant and softly spoken, Williams personifies her project of 'talking about race quietly', though intensity and passion, along with a deep confidence in the power of words, are an evident counterpoint to her mellifluous tones. Equally evident is the fact that, though philosophical about it, she is dispirited by her treatment by the media.

As a law teacher, I am already familiar with the published work which has made Williams one of the best known of the American 'critical race theorists'. Her first book, *The Alchemy of Race and Rights*, uses allegory and metaphor to prompt its readers to meditate on the continuing echoes of

American racism in contemporary law and society. Williams has not only made an important contribution to legal theory but also carved out a genre of rhetoric which is all her own. For these reasons, I am keen to ask her not only about the Reith Lectures but also about the interplay between her intellectual and political commitments and the narrative form in which she typically expresses them.

Williams explains that her project is to illuminate the 'social negotiation of race in small encounters'. She aims to reveal the role of race as an unconscious but powerful element in everyday life, creating misunderstandings and enacting 'micro-aggressions'. Using literary skills, she exposes the 'gaps in perception of the importance of race in the lives of black and white people'. She does not aim to provide a 'grand' theory of racial injustice or oppression; nor does she focus on obvious cases of bigotry and violence. Rather, her approach in these lectures is one of ambitious modesty: to reveal the texture of race in the quotidian encounters of people of good will, with a view to making a 'real, reasoned and nuanced discussion of race' possible.

Williams' conversation, like her writing, is laced with images and stories in which the insights of everyday life, the lessons of history and the commitments of tradition are woven skilfully together. What is controversial about her work is not so much her use of stories but the intellectual context in which she tells them, for her explicitly narrative style poses a challenge to the analytic self-conception of the western academy. She points out that in her days as a trial lawyer, her reasoning by hypotheticals was structurally related to storytelling, emphasising that her work is 'not just storytelling': her stories are designed to prompt a certain line of thought, to open a mental window. As such, both the substance and the structure of her stories are informed by an analysis; and any supposed antinomy between the narrative and the analytic collapses. Conversely, Williams is wary of her reputation as a storyteller — 'gathering you all', she says wryly, 'around my skirts' — resonant as it is with stereotypical images of black women's role in the oral tradition of African-American communities. This is one instance of her general caution about a too-ready romanticism about 'different' traditions, and of her awareness of the risk that an emphasis on the need to respect and accommodate 'difference' can lead to a re-fixing of those marked by difference into stereotyped roles.

In view of some of the more extreme reactions to Williams, it is worth mentioning that the politics of her enterprise are, essentially, an inclusive version of the liberalism that underpinned the American Civil Rights Movement. Williams sees ideals such as 'colour-blindness' as a motivating horizon, notwithstanding the paradoxes set up by the pursuit of colour-blindness in a world in which race structures economic, political and personal life. Her civil rights politics are tempered, however, by a recognition of the need to extend a critical analysis to both unconscious

• • • • • • • • • • • • • • • • • • • • • • • • • • • • • • • • •

**Serious discussion of race has virtually disappeared from British public discourse, surfacing only in spectacular instances where race forces itself onto the media agenda**

• • • • • • • • • • • • • • • • • • • • • • • • • • • • • • • •

and micro-levels. The political and legal strategies she advocates — widened access to the media, expanded forms of public discussion, tolerance and acceptance of multiple voices in political institutions and popular culture, policies of affirmative action — could hardly be said to be revolutionary. What is, however, quietly revolutionary in her thought is the belief that small-scale stories, personal experiences, troubling allegories can serve to make the reality of racism, in Williams' words, 'intimately apparent'. This apparition, in turn, may undermine the accusations and assumptions that have underpinned the backlash against progressive racial politics in the USA.

Why is it, then, that Williams has been portrayed in sections of the British press as a 'militant black feminist who thinks that all whites are racist'? The question prompts some painful reflection on the fact that serious discussion of race has virtually disappeared from British public discourse, surfacing only in spectacular instances where race forces itself onto the media agenda, and where it often meets with sensational rather than considered treatment. The recent debate surrounding the *Daily Mail*'s publication of allegations that five named white men murdered a black teenager, Stephen Lawrence, is instructive here. The case itself reveals the extent to which public institutions have lost their legitimacy in the eyes of ethnic minority groups, and illustrates the threat such a loss of legitimacy poses to civil rights. Significantly, after the initial splash of media outrage on both sides of the debate, the issue — like the recent discussion of the racism of our asylum practices — has once again disappeared from view. It is as if our despair about political solutions in the area of racial injustice generates a resistance to acknowledging its significance. This, perhaps, explains why the press felt so threatened by Williams' very apposite argument, and found it necessary to discredit her views even before they had been properly aired.

Part of the challenge presented by Williams' work lies in the very modesty of her method. As I read her latest book, *The Rooster's Egg*, the weekend before our interview, I have to confess to feeling somewhat ambivalent. I was engaged by the stories, amused by the wit, struck by the images, but uncertain about the conclusions to be drawn. Still musing on the book, I spent Monday evening watching television. Within minutes, I was wincing as Ruby Wax and Sharon Stone joked about mistaking the name of their Chinese hotel waiter (they all look the same...). Half an hour later, I was wincing again, this time at a dialogue in which a BBC journalist suggested to the home secretary that a decisive criticism of the Police Bill was that, as reported in a Turkish newspaper, it instituted surveillance measures more draconian than those in Turkey. To this, the home secretary unhesitatingly retorted that he didn't suppose a Turkish paper understood anything about the proposed legislation. Maybe I would have noticed all this even had *The Rooster's Egg* not been fresh in my mind; then again, maybe I wouldn't. Williams undoubtedly fulfils her ambition to reveal the racially nuanced texture of everyday life. Though the political upshot of her work may as yet be unclear, in a world in which the British prime minister feels able to veto the establishment of a European Union centre to monitor racism and xenophobia, and in which the recent European Youth Survey found that British youth are the most racially intolerant in Europe, we cannot afford to be deaf to one of the most eloquent voices in the struggle against racial injustice. ❏

*Nicola Lacey is professor of law at Birkbeck College, University of London. Parts of this article appeared in the* Times Higher Education Supplement

*Patricia Williams' Reith Lectures,* Seeing a Colour-Blind Future: The Paradox of Race *will be published by Virago in April, price £5.99*

# REVIEW

## JULIAN PETLEY

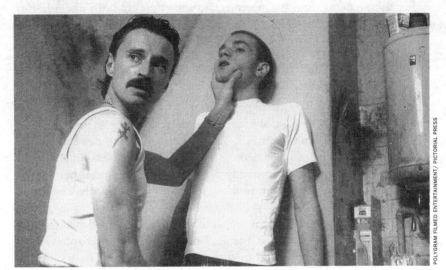

Trainspotting *1996: victim of the moral guardians*

# Doing harm

**The British Board of Film Classification finds itself squeezed by public opinion as the press on the role of censor**

WHEN politicians and press pundits work themselves into a self-righteous frenzy over films such as *Natural Born Killers*, *Child's Play 3* and *Crash* you could easily be forgiven for thinking that Britain has entirely abolished film and video censorship.

Nothing could be further from the truth: Britain inflicts some of the strictest film and video censorship in the western world. Between 1985 and 1995, the British Board of Film Classification cut 23.6 per cent of 18-rated videos and 30.4 per cent of these rated R18. Forty were banned outright. Recent films which have suffered at the hands of the Board, in either their cinema or video versions and sometimes in both, include *Bad Lieutenant*, *Pulp Fiction*, *Dirty Weekend*, *The Good Son*, the James Bond film *Goldeneye*, *Batman Forever*, *Braveheart*, *Die Hard With a Vengeance*, *Under Siege 2*, *Judge Dredd*, *Mortal Kombat*, *Trainspotting*, *Mighty Morphin Power Rangers*, *Showgirls*, *Strange Days*, *True Lies*, *Highlander 3* and *Rob Roy*. In 1995, in the case of cinema films, 15.2 per cent of PGs, 9.3 per cent of 12s, 6.2 per cent of 15s and 1.2 per cent of 18s were passed only after cuts had been made. In the case of videos, the corresponding figures are: PG: 2.1 per cent; 12: 1.1 per cent; 15: 3.4 per cent; 18: 18.4 per cent; R18: 21.7 per cent. Thirty-four videos were cut for reasons of violence and horror, with 84 cuts totalling nearly 35 minutes of running time. A total of 129 sex videos were cut, amounting to some seven and a half hours of sexual activity.

All these details, and many more, can be found in the BBFC's Annual Report 1995-96, published at the end of last year. The Board is often accused of being secretive and of operating behind closed doors; but its Annual Reports are easily available and are a mine of useful information. Last December, the BBFC also published its report to the home secretary Michael Howard, which he had requested following public pronouncements by the widow of the murdered London headmaster Philip Lawrence. As usual, the Annual Report was totally ignored by the press, and the Howard document fared little better. The BBFC's activities are only news, it seems, when there's a lurid (and usually distorted) story to be made out of a *Crash* or *Natural Born Killers*.

Indeed, the role of the press in the censorship process looms large in both reports. As the BBFC points out to Michael Howard, the Board has to 'operate in the real world of popular entertainment, media hype, assorted pressure groups and public alarms'. The press has proved itself particularly effective as a generator of pressure and alarm, and the Annual Report doesn't hesitate to criticise it, in the case of *Natural Born Killers* and *Kids*, for fuelling 'rumours which research proved to be largely untrue'. In the case of *Child's Play 3* and other videos quite wrongly implicated in the James Bulger case, the Report plainly states that the papers have followed James Stewart's advice to a journalist in *The Man Who Shot Liberty Valance*: 'when fact becomes legend, print the legend.' It reserves its strongest condemnation, however, for press behaviour over the *Executions* video (*Index* 4/1995), noting that the press furore played directly into the hands of the distributors who were 'manipulating the news by feeding it with what it wanted, a product trumpeted as suspect, questionable and, best of all, outrageous. Astonishingly the news media rolled over and begged for more, exploiting a news story and being exploited by it. It was a profitable partnership, since not only did it sell videos, but it sold newspapers.'

So, has the BBFC come round to the point of view that lurid stories about 'copycat' crimes sparked off by violence-drenched movies are largely got up by a hypocritical and prurient press? Not quite. For whilst the Board freely admits in both documents that many of the letters of complaint it receives about individual films are from people who have not seen the film but only read press reports about it, it nonetheless tells Howard that such letters 'do measure the temperature of public opinion, and the Board can never ignore such moods, however transitory, since they may well determine the level of public confidence in the Board's decision-making'. In like vein, the Annual Report itself states: 'however little justified by the facts, the fears and anxieties of the public need to be taken seriously, since they create the climate in which films and videos are viewed and judged... The BBFC is faced not just with depictions of violence which worry us, but with the public's perception of that violence, which we must take just as seriously.' And again, talking about the alleged role of *Child's Play 3* in the Bulger murder: 'whether or not these fears were justified, they were plainly real... Legends clearly satisfy a need, and if the culpability of video violence has become a legend, it must be because of the need people feel to fight back against the intrusion into our homes of an unsafe world, replete with danger.'

So having criticised the press for its distortions, the Board then turns round and admits that when these eventually produce equally distorted public perceptions, it acts upon them. Well, here indeed is a 'media effect': film and video censorship in the UK is ultimately dictated by the *Daily Mail* and its ilk.

The BBFC's pusillanimity in this area is all the more puzzling since its report to Michael Howard actually contains some useful snapshots of real public opinion properly gathered, and not populist ranting posing as 'public opinion'. For example, it quotes a 1990 Broadcasting Standards Council survey which found that, although 83 per cent of respondents felt that society was more violent than a decade earlier, 46 per cent put this down to lack of discipline in the home, 21 per cent to unemployment, 14 per cent to lack of discipline in schools and only 12 per cent to television. Video was never cited as a primary cause. In 1991, only eight per cent of complaints to the BBC concerned violence. Meanwhile, in 1996 the BBFC's own Home Viewing Panel ranked violence third (22 per cent) behind drug use (30 per cent) and racism (34 per cent) as areas of 'great concern'. Only nine per cent had seen a video which they considered too violent. Of the same panel, 27 per cent thought that videos were a major factor contributing to violence in society, placing it joint fourth with unemployment but behind lack of discipline/parental control (45 per cent), upbringing/parents/home (39 per cent) and television (33 per cent).

The Board is fond of quoting J S Mill's dictum that 'the only purpose for which power can be rightfully exercised over any member of a civilised community against his will is to prevent harm to others.' This it interprets to mean that the rights of the robust majority to view what it likes must be curtailed to prevent harm to a vulnerable minority. But what if the notion of harm turns out to be untenable, or at least grossly exaggerated? And what of the harm done to freedom of choice and expression, let alone rational debate, by censorship and classification carried out in an air of press-inspired panics? Panics the BBFC itself openly admits are ill-founded but which, at the same time, it treats as a symptom of 'public opinion' rather than dismissing them with the contempt such populist antics deserve. ❏

*Julian Petley is head of communication and information studies at Brunel University, UK. He is co-editor of* Ill Effects: The Media Violence Debate *(Routledge 1997, £12.99pb, £40hb)*

---

**Correction** *In the article by Han Dongfang 'A voice for the millions' (Index 1/1997) the sentence on page 84, 'We want to serve as an opposition party tool', should have read 'We do not want to serve as an opposition party tool'. We apologise for this unfortunate typo.*

---

*After the riot...burned-out church, Situbondo, East Java 1996 Credit: ABS*

# Spontaneous combustion

The recent eruption of religious, ethnic and social turmoil in Indonesia poses the most serious challenge yet to the 32-year rule of President Suharto's New Order. General elections in May hold no promise of change: the government, backed by the army, maintains a tight grip on power and ruthlessly suppresses dissent. But what happens to those who refuse to toe the official line?

A special report compiled with the help of the Institut Studi Arus Informasi (Institute for the Studies on Free Flow of Information), Jakarta and with the financial support of the Norwegian Foreign Ministry

# Indonesia: fact file

Area: more than 17,000 islands (of which 6,000 are inhabited) with a total land mass of 1.9 million sq km
Total population: 197.6 million, making it the fourth most populous country in the world
Population of East Timor: 826,000
Number of East Timorese who have died as a result of war, famine, disease and extrajudicial execution since Indonesia invaded in 1975: 200,000 (one-third of the pre-invasion population)
Population density in Java and Madura: 859.3 per sq km
   in Bali: 517.8 per sq km
   in Irian Jaya: 4.5 per sq km
Birth rate in Indonesia: 24 per 1,000
   in East Timor: 44.2 per 1,000
Death rate in Indonesia: 8 per 1,000
   in East Timor: 21.5 per 1,000
Life expectancy in Indonesia: 62 for women, 58.5 for men
   in East Timor: 43.4 for women, 42.4 for men

Unit of currency: Rupiah (Rp)
Exchange rate: US$1 = Rp 2,246
GDP: Rp 363,014 billion (US$168 billion)
Origins of GDP: 22.3% manufacturing, 18.5% agriculture, 16.5% trade, 10.2% mining
GDP per capita: US$883
GDP growth rate: 7.3%
Principal trading partner: Japan

The five principles of the official state ideology, Pancasila: 1) belief in a monotheistic god; 2) just and civilised humanity; 3) the unity of Indonesia; 4) democracy guided by wisdom and deliberation among representatives; 5) social justice for all Indonesians

Number of recognised religions: Five — Islam (86.9%), Protestantism and Catholicism (9.6%), Hinduism (1.9%), Buddhism (1%), Confucianism (0.6%). Mystical tribal religions (0.5%) such as Aliran Kepercayaan are also tolerated. All citizens must state their religion

Number of recognised languages: over 450 (270 Austronesian languages and 180 Papuan)
Number of languages with more than a million speakers: 13
National language: Bahasa Indonesia

Proportion of children in primary education (age 6-13): 97%
in secondary education (age 13-19): 37%
Proportion of children in full-time work: 4% (a further 4% work and attend school)
Adult literacy: 81.6% (88.3% male, 75.3% female)

Number of licensed newspapers and magazines: 200 (including 68 dailies with total circulation of 15 million)
Number of unlicensed newspapers and magazines: over 300
People who own a television: 9 million (the number of viewers is estimated at 90 million)
People who own a radio: 40 million
There is one state-controlled TV station (TVR1) and five commercial stations
The state-controlled radio network includes 50 local and 150 municipal government stations. There are also 600 privately owned radio stations
In 1992, 6,303 books published
In 1989, 104 films were made in Indonesia. In 1996, there were 38.

Officially reported number of cases of AIDS: 108
WHO's estimate of number of people with HIV: 95,000

Sources: Article 19, Catholic Institute for International Relations, Economist Intelligence Unit, Europa — Far East and Australasia 1996, World Health Organisation

# MARGOT COHEN

# Climate of distrust

**By the year 2020 Indonesia will be the world's fifth largest economy, according to the latest World Bank forecast. But an upsurge in religious and ethnic violence is threatening to undermine the stability which is essential for future prosperity**

O N a rugged beach off the coast of West Java, a man on a horse motioned to his troops with a sharp jab of a sword. 'God is great!' he thundered, wheeling around to lead the midnight charge against the enemy. In bare feet and white turbans, the men raced across the sand, certain that their Islamic faith would ensure glory and honour.

Could this be a scene from 1997? Yes and no. It's a snippet from the 200 cans of film shot on location this year for *Fatahillah*, a historical epic set in the fifteenth century. Yet it also provides a glimpse into modern-day religious politics under President Suharto's New Order government.

By Hollywood standards, *Fatahillah*'s budget of three billion rupiah (US$1.3 million) is peanuts, but this story of a Muslim hero battling Portuguese colonisers is the most expensive movie ever made in Indonesia. Harmoko, Indonesia's information minister and chairman of the ruling party, Golkar, is credited with hatching the idea — and even stepped in as movie director for a day.

*Fatahillah* is a graphic sign of the growing rapprochement between the Suharto government and Indonesia's Islamic community. Muslims account for approximately 87 per cent of the population, but relations between various Muslim groups and the government have previously been tense, with Islamic separatism seen as a threat to national unity. However, the late 1980s ushered in a new era. With Suharto relying on Muslim groups to broaden his power base, the government has encouraged Muslim think-tanks, publications, banks and schools. Trade links with Muslim countries are growing. This has all fostered a national atmosphere of Islamic pride, displayed in bumper stickers such as 'Islam is my blood' and 'Islam is the truth.' Veteran film director Chaerul Umam observes that it would have been difficult to make *Fatahillah* in the early days of the New Order. 'Now the government is creating opportunities for Muslims in a very positive way,' he says.

Still, it would be wrong to suggest that *Fatahillah* marks the beginning of an epic Holy War in Indonesia. Civilian and military leaders both recognise that growing Muslim pride must be matched by strong commitment to religious tolerance in order to preserve unity. Indonesia is not a Muslim nation. The state recognises five religions: Catholicism, Protestantism, Hinduism, Buddhism and Islam.

There is no question that economic prosperity remains contingent on an atmosphere of mutual tolerance and respect. Religious strife might scare off foreign investors, who have been helping Indonesia's economy grow by seven to eight per cent each year. Domestically, the ethnic Chinese control an estimated 70 per cent of the country's private economy, although they represent just three per cent of the population. While there are Muslim Chinese preachers who are building a higher profile, most of the country's ethnic Chinese adhere to Christianity, Buddhism or Confucianism. (The last is not a state-approved religion, however, which has caused problems in obtaining marriage permits.)

In light of the religious and ethnic conflicts that have erupted in countries such as India and the former Yugoslavia, Indonesia has done a remarkable job in weaving its diverse islands and peoples into one nation. One important tool has been the national language, Bahasa Indonesia, vigorously promoted through state television and public education.

In recent months, however, this carefully-woven national fabric has started to fray. Once-unfamiliar names such as Rengasdengklok, Sanggau Ledo, Tasikmalaya, and Situbondo have flared into notoriety as sites of riots with ethnic and religious overtones. Targets have included churches, temples, shops, police stations, factories, and vehicles. Since October last year, more than a dozen people have died in riots on the island of Java, according to official estimates. Hundreds — possibly thousands — more are thought to have been killed in the grisly ethnic clash between Dayaks and Madurese in West Kalimantan in February.

This seeming epidemic of violence has prompted a fair amount of soul-searching among Indonesians of all social classes. It has also prompted a rash of conspiracy theories among those eager to sniff out any national political implications. Facts are fuzzy; speculation rife. But as the incidents mount, one thing is becoming startlingly clear: rumour maintains a powerful hold on the imagination of many Indonesians. It is hard to avoid the conclusion that people's trust in official channels of communication has ebbed.

Take the case of Situbondo, the East Java town where the first of the latest string of riots occurred. On the surface, it appeared to be confined to the Islamic community. A Muslim crowd had gathered at a local courthouse to witness another Muslim being sentenced for heresy. Then

● ● ● ● ● ● ● ● ● ● ● ● ● ● ● ● ● ● ● ● ● ● ● ● ● ● ● ● ● ● ● ●

**Some point to the rapid spread of destruction as evidence of a 'hidden hand'. But even the most ardent conspiracy theorists concede that very real conflicts are brewing at the grassroots**

● ● ● ● ● ● ● ● ● ● ● ● ● ● ● ● ● ● ● ● ● ● ● ● ● ● ● ● ● ● ● ●

the rumour broke that the defendant was hiding out in a local church. Boom. By the time the dust had cleared, 21 churches had been desecrated.

In Tasikmalaya, in West Java, local Muslims were furious that three teachers of religion had been beaten by local police. Suddenly the rumour leaked that one of the teachers had died. Boom. Seventeen police stations trashed, five churches burned.

In Ngarak, West Kalimantan, angry Dayak villagers refused to believe military officers who said that rumours about the murder of a Dayak leader were untrue. The leader had to be transported to Ngarak by helicopter to reassure the villagers he was alive and well. Even so, the Dayaks tried to push past a military barricade in their eagerness to avenge other relatives believed to have been killed by Madurese. The result was a fresh batch of corpses.

Many observers point to the rapid spread of destruction as evidence that the riots are being guided by an 'unseen hand', or perhaps two or three different 'unseen hands'. This view is bolstered by historical evidence of Indonesian government intelligence agents stirring up trouble for political ends. Even the most ardent conspiracy theorists, however, concede that very real conflicts are brewing at the grassroots. The Suharto government has been quite successful in throwing open the door to primary and secondary school education, but less successful in generating jobs to accommodate all the fresh graduates. Under-employment, estimated at 30 per cent in some academic circles, fuels resentment of the industrious ethnic Chinese community. Since the ethnic Chinese are seen primarily as non-Muslim, economic frustration can easily boil over into religious prejudice and, ultimately, violence.

While rapid development has been a source of pride, it has also served to displace communities and wreak havoc with traditional economic relationships. Major infrastructure and industrial projects have sent villagers scuttling to put down new roots. Small shopkeepers are watching long-time customers rush off to supermarkets and malls to spend their pay. When the money runs out towards the end of the month, however, these same customers rely on the trusty shopkeepers to extend credit. And so the burden grows.

In this climate of rapid change, religion acts as both salve and irritant. It's not just something to hold on to, but something that threatens to slip away. Indonesians of all religious persuasions are keeping score of conversions. They remain on the lookout for schools and hospitals that display missionary zeal. Intermarriage is loudly deplored at religious gatherings. The matter is so sensitive that the Ministry of Religion no longer releases official figures on the religious breakdown of the population. A few percentage points could spell very big trouble.

Some Indonesian Christians complain that their Muslim compatriots are a 'numerical majority with a minority complex'. As the Suharto government has drawn closer to Muslim groups, Christians say it has become harder to obtain government permits to build new churches. Some Christian congregations, fed up after waiting two years or more, decide to go ahead and establish 'storefront' churches anyway. These unlicensed churches then become even more vulnerable to Muslim community wrath. Such was the case in Pasuruan, East Java, where the home of a Pentecostal preacher was burnt down in 1992.

But the permit problem is not confined to Christians. In 1995, for example, the chairman of Muhammadiyah, one of Indonesia's largest Muslim organisations, complained that it was too difficult for Muslims to establish new mosques in East Timor, where the majority of the population is Catholic. The difference is clout. The Muhammadiyah official was also a prominent leader of the Indonesian Association of

Muslim Intellectuals, a new Muslim think-tank close to the ruling elite. Shortly after the complaint was aired, East Timor's governor was forced to change the rules to make it easier to build new mosques.

Meanwhile, a host of anonymous pamphlets and flyers are fanning religious prejudice. Titles such as 'Working Programme to Christianise Indonesia' pack an emotional punch, no matter how illogical the content. It can be argued that the government's crackdown on the mainstream press — such as the 1994 banning of the news magazines *Tempo*, *Editor* and *DeTik* — has unwittingly added an air of credibility to these anonymous tracts. Continuing state censorship of radio, television, and newspapers has enforced the image that 'real' information exists only outside formal channels.

In January this year, Armed Forces chief Feisal Tanjung announced that the military is to set up a network of 'National Vigilance Posts' to seek out and quash rumours that might otherwise lead to religious and ethnic tensions. The posts, in effect, represent a new layer of intelligence activity across the country, suggesting that previous military intelligence reports have been inadequate or unreliable. Pro-democracy activists worry that the military posts will only serve as new instruments of repression. They maintain that the ruling party, Golkar, wishes to tighten its grip on the grassroots population in the run-up to legislative elections in May. However, military officers insist they are looking to foster dialogue, not fear. Religious and community leaders are expected to play an active role in these posts. How well they communicate with each other — and their followers — will determine the nature and effectiveness of the new network.

Clearly, Indonesia will have a tough time overcoming the current wave of violence unless the nation's rulers openly face the problems lurking beneath the triumphant tide of gains in development. In navigating the seas of religious and economic insecurities, however, Indonesia can look around the world and take comfort from the fact that it is not alone. ❏

*Margot Cohen* is a journalist based in Jakarta

# SANTOSO

*Jakarta 1996: Troops march past under the watchful eye of President Suharto*

# Portents of change

In May, Indonesia celebrates its 'festival of democracy', as the government calls the elections. The political system is carefully loaded to guarantee that Golkar, the ruling party, cannot lose. But there are signs that a major change is on the way

PEOPLE know that the legislative elections, scheduled for 29 May, will have little impact on their lives. Under the Constitution, ultimate power rests with the People's Consultative Assembly (MPR). This is the body that elects the president and, in name anyway, determines state policy. Of its 1,000 members, only 425 are actually chosen by the people in the general election — the rest are appointed by the president. An MPR whose majority has been chosen by a president is likely to re-elect the same person to continue in that post. For the 32 years of the New Order regime, Indonesia has only ever had one candidate for the post of president, 75-year-old Suharto. Come 1998, he is likely to be elected for a sixth time.

Since the New Order government came to power in 1965 — after the struggle between the army and the Indonesian Communist Party (PKI) which ended in the murder, imprisonment and deportation of hundreds of thousands of people who were suspected of being Communist party members or sympathisers — there have been five general elections, all of them won by the government party, Golkar, with between 62 and 73 per cent of the popular vote. In the coming elections, Golkar says it is aiming for 70 per cent, a target that won't be hard to achieve given the way the electoral system works.

All aspects of the electoral process are effectively under the control of Golkar and the state bureaucracy. To start with, only three parties are permitted to contest elections: Golkar, the Muslim United Development Party (PPP) and the Indonesian Democratic Party (PDI). The last two operate at a severe disadvantage. The policy known as 'floating mass' forbids them from organising at village level. By contrast, because all of the country's 3.5 million civil servants (who include village heads) are obliged to belong to Golkar, that party's organisational reach extends right down to village level. Not only that, but the bureaucrats also run and monitor all aspects of the electoral process. This structural imbalance guarantees that Golkar has no meaningful competition for votes.

Although neither the PDI nor the PPP has any real chance of power, the New Order regime denies them full independence, repeatedly interfering in their internal affairs. The removal in June last year of Megawati Soekarnoputri as chair of the PDI, and her replacement with a pro-government functionary, was a clear example of the government's determination to rein in her party. Ever since her election as PDI leader in 1993, the eldest daughter of ex-President Soekarno has been regarded with deep suspicion by the government. When some of her supporters proposed that she stand as a presidential candidate in 1998 — a political move unheard of in the New Order — Megawati was promptly toppled. The subsequent police takeover of the PDI's headquarters on 27 July last year led to the worst rioting that the country has seen for many years.

Stability is at the heart of New Order politics. Everything is geared towards maintaining stability at any cost. The Indonesian Armed Forces (ABRI) is the backbone of the system, but not everything depends on the threat of force. Through the long-established doctrine of 'dual function', which gives the army both security and political roles, ABRI plays a key part in social and political life. With an allocation of 100 seats in the MPR (to be reduced to 75 after the forthcoming elections), ABRI has long regarded itself as having the right to take a stance on controversial political issues — for example, specifying what news may be published by the mass media, being actively involved in land clearances or breaking up labour strikes.

The New Order's veneration for stability has one clear and overriding aim: economic development. And, as various economic indicators demonstrate, the New Order has met with some striking successes. Over the past 25 years, economic growth has averaged 6.8 per cent a year. The average annual income, which stood at just US$50 in 1965, has now reached US$1,000. Since 1984 Indonesia has not had to import rice to meet its needs. And between 1971 and 1995, literacy rose from 60 per cent to 86 per cent.

These successes, however, have a price: a complete lack of public accountability, leading to corruption and nepotism on a massive scale. Soemitro Djojohadikusumo, one of the architects of the New Order's economic policies, has admitted that a staggering 30 per cent of the state budget is prone to what is euphemistically called 'leakage'. This means that, out of the 1997-98 budget of Rp 100 trillion, some Rp 30 trillion (over US$13 billion) will be siphoned off. But even this is dwarfed by the amounts creamed off from the government's 'unofficial' funds, the part of its budget that is not open to parliamentary scrutiny. The economist Hartojo Wignjowijoto estimates that these funds could amount to as much as *three times* the official budget. If that is accurate, corruption levels in 1997-98 could be as high as US$52 billion — more than the entire official state budget.

Nepotism among the political elite is a very familiar story to

● ● ● ● ● ● ● ● ● ● ● ● ● ● ● ● ● ● ● ● ● ● ● ● ● ● ● ● ●

## SARAH SMITH

# An elastic law

Indonesia's anti-subversion law was introduced by presidential decree in 1963 and formally enacted two years later by President Suharto, who used the new code to crush the banned Communist Party of Indonesia (PKI). Although infrequently invoked, it has a wide remit and its terminology is so vague as to leave any expression of dissent open to prosecution.

The law carries a maximum penalty of death and covers 'whosoever has engaged in an action with the purpose of [subversion], or clearly with the purpose which is known to him, or which can be expected to be known to him.' It criminalises any act which could distort, undermine or deviate from Pancasila ideology or state policy; or which could disseminate feelings of hostility or arouse hostility, disturbances or anxiety among the population. It enables charges to be brought on the slightest of evidence and the standards of proof required for conviction are less rigorous than those for other types of offence.

The anti-subversion law has been criticised in recent years by Indonesia's National Commission on Human Rights for its 'elasticity'. The death penalty, too, has come to be seen as inconsistent with the Pancasila principle of humanitarianism (out of 39 people executed since 1978, 30 were political prisoners convicted for links with the 1965 coup attempt and/or membership of the PKI. Nearly 30 years after being convicted, four PKI prisoners remain on death row). In 1993 the Agency for the Development of National Law drafted a bill to replace the criminal code, which would render the anti-subversion law obsolete. It has yet to be brought before the House of Representatives, however.

Between 250 and 350 people are believed to be serving sentences for subversion, including PKI members, Muslim militants and members of the Irian Jaya, Aceh and East Timor separatist movements. Thirteen people are currently standing trial for subversion in connection with the Jakarta riots (with another two expected to be indicted soon), while ousted PDI leader Megawati Soekarnoputri has been summoned for questioning under the law in connection with a meeting in January this year (see page 88).

● ● ● ● ● ● ● ● ● ● ● ● ● ● ● ● ● ● ● ● ● ● ● ● ● ● ● ● ●

Indonesians. The president's family has extensive financial interests in the country's mining and oil industries. But the world at large was given a particularly blatant example of it when the government announced its new strategy for the 'national car'. President Suharto's son Tommy was given major tax breaks (which were denied to his competitors) to enable him to set up a car manufacturer in partnership with the South Korean company KIA. Indonesia came in for a hail of criticism from abroad, and complaints were lodged with the World Trade Organisation.

Tommy's choice of name for the national car — the 'Timor' — was a bitter irony. Officials have always sought to play down the importance of the East Timor question, but the award last year of the Nobel peace prize to the Bishop of Dili, Carlos Felipe Ximenes Belo, and José Ramos-Horta, leader-in-exile of the East Timor independence movement, was a slap in the face for the government. The New Order persists with the line that the 'integration' of East Timor into Indonesia is final and irrevocable, partly perhaps due to a reluctance to admit having done wrong in invading the Portuguese colony in the first place. A more compelling reason is the island's tremendous business potential. With revenues from the coffee and marble trades beginning to flow into the pockets of Jakarta-based businesses, not to mention the potential of pearl beds and oil fields, any resolution for the East Timor issue is only going to become more difficult.

In defence of its stand on East Timor, the New Order argues that it has achieved more development in the last 22 years than Portugal did in 200. They cite the building of markets, bridges, hospitals, almost 2,500 kilometres of roads and a university as evidence of a commitment to improving the lives of the people of East Timor. Yet all this has failed to secure East Timorese acceptance of integration. The Dili demonstration in November 1991, in which more than 250 people were killed by the security forces, was organised by the very people — the young — who have grown up amidst this development and benefited most from it. 'If you're only talking about development,' says the jailed East Timorese resistance leader Xanana Gusmão (see page 51), 'then South Africa also developed Namibia. Israel also developed Palestine. The problem of colonialism is not a question of whether or not there is development.'

There is a feeling of guilt now emerging among Indonesians about what the New Order has done in East Timor, which will only increase the demands for peaceful resolution of the issue. In fact, the East Timor question is intimately bound up with the process of democratisation in Indonesia, because the more that Indonesians demand their full democratic rights, the more it opens up the possibility of a referendum in East Timor. And the pressure for democracy is currently building up in all aspects of life. The response to censorship of the printed media has been a flourishing of unlicensed publications. The ban on establishing new political parties, besides the three formally permitted, has been flouted: the People's Democratic Party (PRD) and the Indonesian United Democratic Party have both been set up despite being deemed illegal and being denied the right to take part in

*Bishop Carlos Belo of Dili*

elections. And NGO activists, intellectuals, mass social and religious organisations stood shoulder to shoulder in organising the Independent Election Monitoring Committee (KIPP) to analyse the conduct of the May elections — the first time anything like this has been attempted under the New Order.

The riots that hit Jakarta in July last year signalled a growing rejection of the existing political order. The spectre of Communism, which the government has long used to frighten the public into submission, has lost its power. Even when President Suharto insisted that the riots had been instigated by people with 'PKI mentalities' and then declared the masterminds to be Maoists, no-one really believed him. Previously, when he talked in such terms, no-one dared to express a different point of view. Now things are different. The New Order's power has entered its twilight era and society's patience with the harshness of this regime is exhausted. Major change is coming to Indonesia — but not through these elections.❏

*Santoso is secretary-general of the Alliance of Independent Journalists (AJI)*

# East Timor's path to peace

The brutality of Indonesia's record in East Timor is undeniable: a third of the population dead since the 1975 invasion, hundreds killed by security forces in the 1991 Dili massacre, scores of arbitrary arrests and extrajudicial executions currently being committed in Viqueque, Liquiçá and Dili. In light of that, any hope of freedom for the former Portuguese colony might seem remote. Yet efforts are being made to resolve the situation.

The most far-ranging and detailed proposals for peace in East Timor are those put forward by the pro-independence National Council for Maubere Resistance (CNRM). Their three-phase initiative allows a timetable of up to 12 years for a transition to self-determination. Phase one deals with the reduction of Indonesia's military and administrative presence, and their replacement by UN agencies. This would coincide with the removal of restrictions on the media, on political activity and on the teaching of Portuguese. Phase two involves the establishment of a political infrastructure to work towards autonomy. The normalisation of relations between Indonesia and Portugal is also envisaged. And phase three leads to full self-determination, mandated if necessary by a UN-administered referendum.

Five years after it was first put forward, Indonesia has made no response to the CNRM plan. But there are other paths towards peace. A first step towards wide-ranging talks was taken in 1995, when the UN set up the All-Inclusive Intra-East Timorese Dialogue. The agenda included demilitarisation, human rights and power transfer to civilian authorities. However, the Indonesian delegates were regarded by Jakarta as having conceded too much in the talks, and were forced to renounce the final declaration which recognised East Timor's right to self-determination. A follow-up meeting, in March last year, was less productive, concentrating mainly on keeping the process itself alive.

Another possibility is tripartite talks under the aegis of the UN, involving both Indonesia and Portugal, and the two countries have been discussing ways in which diplomatic relations could be upgraded. Here too, however, there is a vast gulf to be bridged. Yet opinion in Portugal and East Timor seems to suggest that time is on their side: the constant drip of international condemnation, plus uncertainty over the nature of a post-Suharto Indonesia might yet add up to a genuine sea-change in East Timor's fortunes. *AN*

# XANANA GUSMÃO

# Eyes on the prize

*The thousands of people who welcomed Nobel prize-winner Bishop Carlos Belo back to Dili on 24 December were also carrying posters of Xanana Gusmão. The charismatic former leader of the Revolutionary Front for an Independent East Timor (Fretilin) has been in prison in Jakarta since 1992, serving a 20-year sentence for rebellion and possession of firearms. Gusmão, a poet and former seminary student, spent 11 years leading the armed resistance in the Timorese jungle. In 1989 he became leader of the National Council of Maubere Resistance (CNRM), a newly formed alliance of pro-independence groups. 'Maubere' is a name adopted by Fretilin to signify 'the oppressed'. Below are excerpts from conversations with Gusmão in Cipinang prison over the last Christmas holidays*

'IT IS perfectly fitting that Bishop Belo and José Ramos Horta were awarded the Nobel peace prize. They represent the aspirations of the people who, throughout this prolonged conflict, have craved a true and lasting peace.

'In our struggle, in which the Maubere people are few and lack the strength to oppose the power of a modern military, the moral aspect plays a very important role. Even minor victories encourage the 'fighting spirit' which breathes life into the national consciousness of our people. The Nobel prize is an international acknowledgement of our struggle. Because of that, our people see this Nobel peace prize as a sign that their sacrifices have not been in vain.

'The basic problem in East Timor is that there is no single international solution which is acceptable to all sides. Jakarta always rejects our peace proposals for illogical, apparently stupid, reasons. Human rights violations continue to be a serious issue, because the most fundamental human rights violation is the violation of the right of our people to decide their own fate. The East Timorese people have never been given the freedom to say freely what it is they want for their political future. Other problems follow from the illegal and criminal military occupation. The problem is not the lack of freedom in itself, but what causes that lack of freedom.

'What happened to [the banned news weeklies] *Tempo*, *Editor* and *DeTik* really brought home to me the situation of the media in Indonesia. The days of professional and independent journalists are gone and all we see now is political subservience. I believe that the Indonesian press feels that it has failed to accomplish its mission in society and has ruined its reputation. I have followed the case of *Tempo* and, more closely still, the PDI case. I saw the disappointment of *Media Indonesia* readers when the paper was forbidden to write about Megawati. The Indonesian press's room for manoeuvre these days is about as wide as my prison cell.

'If you read the CNRM peace plan you will see the kind of freedom we want for East Timor. The issue of a referendum is the principal one, and there cannot be a truly just solution if UN norms are not applied. But even supposing the East Timorese people chose integration, there won't be any freedom there if the Indonesian people continue to be oppressed and denied their freedom. The referendum must be carried out under the aegis of the UN and international supervision in order to prevent it from becoming a farce, like elections in Indonesia. With the forthcoming elections, for example, the comedy started last year with the ouster of Megawati by that clown Soerjadi [the government-backed replacement leader of the PDI], the arrest of the PRD people and with the judicial review of Muchtar Pakpahan's case by the prosecutor, and so on (see p88).

'The Indonesian government is really afraid of me speaking the truth and explaining to the Indonesian people why the annexation of East Timor is illegal and criminal. What surprises me is that the government knows that what I say will never be published inside Indonesia. But even so they are afraid of me, in the same way that they are afraid of Ali Sadikin, Gus Dur, Sri Bintang, Megawati, Aditjondro and all their critics who honestly wish to see political change in this country.' ❏

*For more information on East Timor, contact the East Timor Project, c/o CIIR, Unit 3, Canonbury Yard, 190A New North Road, London N1 7BJ, UK Tel: +44 171 354 0883; fax: +44 171 359 0017*

# ANDREAS HARSONO

# On the line

**Government control over the media is absolute and unyielding — and woe betide those who overstep the mark**

'IT IS dangerous to be right,' wrote Voltaire, 'when the government is wrong' — to which most Indonesian journalists would probably reply that in their experience it is better to be pragmatic, even to report lies, than to tell the truth. 'If you write something the government doesn't approve of, they call up the chief editor and tell you to stick to the official press releases. We call it the "telephone culture",' explains a journalist working for an Indonesian business daily.

And the threats don't only come by phone. In June last year chief editors in Jakarta were called in by a military official and encouraged to support the government's overthrow of Megawati Soekarnoputri, the eldest daughter of former President Soekarno and a popular political figure. They were also told not to use the term 'ousted' when describing the government's removal and replacement of her as chair of the PDI. Editors were also warned against using Megawati's surname because of its association with her father, and were advised instead to call her by her husband's name.

Even greater media engineering took place in the case of the new, but formally unrecognised, People's Democratic Party (PRD). A week before the Jakarta riots of 27 July, an ABRI (armed forces) official did the rounds of the editorial offices, providing information about the PRD which, he claimed, proved the organisation's Communist leanings. The official urged editors and producers to use the information. The highly damaging — and unproven — accusations duly made headlines in both the print and broadcast media, and provided the basis for official charges that the following week's disturbances were mainly orchestrated by the PRD.

Thirty years after he gained power following the abortive coup d'etat of 1965, President Suharto has transformed this nation into a very carefully balanced political system defined by an invisible line of tolerance. Old editorial hands say that on the forbidden side of this invisible line lie the personal lives of the Suharto family (whose business empires have grown tremendously because of their patriarch's position), East Timor, human rights violations in general and Megawati Soekarnoputri. 'When we're writing about East Timor we have to use the word "integration" instead of "invasion",' says another journalist. 'Writing the wrong word means your editor barking at you and questioning your patriotism.'

The government has also introduced a group of media taboos known collectively by the acronym SARA: '*Suku*' (ethnicity), '*Agama*' (religion), '*Ras*' (race) and '*Antar golongan*' (inter-community). When dozens of churches were burned down by Muslim protesters in the towns of Situbondo and Tasikmalaya in 1996 the daily paper *Kompas*, which has strong Catholic connections, used the term 'houses of worship' rather than 'churches'. This is a SARA issue and the newspaper does not want to be seen to be highlighting religious tensions.

Perhaps the most important example, however, came in 1994, when several papers reported a dispute among aides to President Suharto over the procurement of 39 warships from the former East German navy. Research and technology minister B J Habibie requested US$1.1 billion to buy and to renovate the ships. His rivals, who include several military generals and finance minister Mar'ie Muhammad, refused to sanction such expenditure, and slashed the budget to US$300 million. The generals complained that they could not use the Soviet-modelled ships because their sailors are more familiar with western equipment. 'You cannot go to war with your admirals unable to read the Russian instructions,' said one military analyst.

The media thought the story merited publication. It involved some big names, money, politics, manoeuvring and friction among powerful officials. It turned out to be an expensive, indeed lethal, decision. Suharto accused the media of pitting government officials against one another. Worse than that, Indonesia's number one man, himself a former military commander, ordered the closure of *Tempo*, *DeTik* and *Editor* news weeklies. A government official explained that 'the government had been forced to revoke the publishing licences of the three magazines for the sake of the development of a free, healthy and responsible press, and for the sake of national stability.'

At the time, the weeklies were the three biggest political magazines in the country. *Tempo* was launched in 1971 and modelled on *Time* magazine. When the government closed it down in June 1994, *Tempo* had 400 staff, sales of about 200,000 and a readership estimated at 1.4 million. The banning of the weeklies was the death knell for freedom of the press in Indonesia.

Aside from banning newspapers and arresting journalists — the most visible aspect of its repressive policies — the government has two other sophisticated weapons to bring the media into the line. The first is the state-sanctioned Association of Indonesian Journalists (PWI), which acts as the official watchdog in editorial offices. The PWI can revoke its endorsement of an editor, automatically prompting the government to ban his newspaper. Information minister Harmoko, the man who introduced this system, usually appoints his cronies to fill strategic positions in the PWI. Sofjan Lubis, the PWI's president, is the chief editor of the Jakarta-based daily *Pos Kota*, which is owned by Harmoko. Meanwhile, Tarman Azzam, the editor of its sister paper *Harian Terbit*, heads the PWI's Jakarta branch. Harmoko has also issued a decree making it compulsory for Indonesian journalists — whether working for domestic or foreign news organisations — to become members of the PWI.

The second weapon is the system of publishing licences, commonly known by its acronym, SIUPP. A licence can be revoked at any time, thereby enabling Harmoko (who also chairs the ruling party, Golkar), to create a system of self-censorship that generates fear among journalists. Although the 1982 Press Law specifically prohibits censorship or bans, Harmoko has issued another ministerial decree allowing the government to revoke publishing licences on editorial grounds. He insists that revocation is totally different from banning.

As the May elections draw nearer, the government is trying to tighten its grip on the media in order to gain as much control as possible of campaign coverage. The two officially recognised opposition parties, the PPP and the PDI, have repeatedly asked the state-owned television station, TVRI, to be fair when covering political parties' activities. Harmoko, clad in his yellow Golkar uniform, appears daily on TVRI. Opposition leaders say they can accept the fact that private stations might choose to give more coverage to Golkar than to the opposition, but TVRI is not owned by Golkar — it is owned by the public.

## SANTOSO

# Murder, corruption and lies

Fuad Muhammad Syafruddin

Last August, on the eve of the anniversary of independence, the murder of a journalist shook the nation. Fuad Muhammad Syafruddin, known as Udin, was attacked and brutally beaten in his home by two men, and died three days later. Udin was a journalist with *Bernas*, a local newspaper published in Yogyakarta. Despite considerable pressure from local officials, he exposed corruption in a local village development fund and electioneering irregularities by Golkar. Most importantly, Udin revealed that the regent of Bantul had promised a bribe of Rp 1 billion (US$430,000) to a foundation chaired by President Suharto in order to ensure his re-election.

Before he died, Udin received telephone threats from the local military warning him to halt his investigations. He refused. So when Udin was murdered, apparently

Indonesia's five private TV stations are no more independent, since they are owned by the children and associates of the president. The largest of them, RCTI, is part of Bimantara Citra business group controlled by Suharto's son Bambang Trihatmodjo. His elder sister, Siti Hardiyanti Rukmana, known as 'Sister Tutut', controls the station TPI, while SCTV is supported by a financial consortium which includes Suharto's cousin Sudwikatmono. AN-teve, meanwhile, is controlled by Golkar politician Agung Laksono. The newest of the five, Indosiar, belongs to the Salim group which is owned by a long-standing friend of Suharto, businessman Liem Sioe Liong. Government control of private broadcasting is made absolute by the fact that, like the printed media, the stations have to by professional killers, there was a strong suspicion that it had been ordered by someone who had been angered by his work. These suspicions were confirmed when a senior military officer acknowledged that the regent of Bantul had admitted to having ordered Udin beaten — apparently to 'teach him a lesson' — although he denied wanting him killed.

Despite this admission, the regent has yet to be questioned. Indeed the police repeatedly denied the possibility of a political motive for Udin's death, and instead arrested Dwi Sumaji, a young driver, whom they accused of murdering Udin in revenge for a supposed affair with Dwi's wife. The police case was considerably weakened by testimony from Udin's wife, who saw her husband's killers, that Dwi Sumaji was not one of them. And when the circumstances of Dwi's arrest and confession were revealed, any credibility the police may still have had was lost. It turned out that they had plied Dwi with drink, hired him a prostitute, and promised him gifts if he admitted to Udin's murder. Once he sobered up, Dwi retracted his 'confession'.

Amazingly, the police have taken their case to court. It looks as if the injustice of Udin's murder will be compounded by the imprisonment of an innocent man. Meanwhile, high-ranking government officials are trying to distance themselves from the case, denying all knowledge of the regent's bribe to the president's foundation. Instead a new scenario is being put forward to muddy the waters, in which the regent is portrayed as having been the victim of blackmail. Few are buying it. But this case involves powerful people and, in such cases, power invariably wins out.

● ● ● ● ● ● ● ● ● ● ● ● ● ● ● ● ● ● ● ● ● ● ● ● ● ● ● ● ● ● ● ● ●

obtain broadcasting licences which must be renewed every five years and can be cancelled at any time.

Fear among Indonesian journalists has increased over the past couple of years. The government now controls almost every aspect of the mass media. Although journalists here know that the government is wrong, the government is also very powerful. The question therefore is whether those journalists who have been advocating greater freedom for the press can maintain the energy to resist. Win or lose, they face a long and dangerous fight. ❏

*Andreas Harsono* *is a journalist and secretary-general of ISAI*

● ● ● ● ● ● ● ● ● ● ● ● ● ● ● ● ● ● ● ● ● ● ● ● ● ● ● ● ● ● ● ● ●

# SANTOSO

# Into cyberspace

So far the Internet has been beyond the reach of state censorship. Since the 1994 bannings, Internet users have multiplied in Indonesia, with an estimated 100,000 now online. When the mainstream media became too frightened to report the facts, the Internet became an efficient alternative. It not only provides uncensored news but has also become a forum for heated debate on sensitive topics avoided by the mass media, like religion, race or presidential issues. During and after last July's riots in Jakarta, while all of the mainstream media waited for official guidance, the Internet became the fastest source of accurate information.

The increasing number of Internet users inspired the growth of cyberspace news agencies, for example Tempo Interaktif (http://www.tempo.co.id/), run by former *Tempo* journalists who are banned from working in the mainstream media. The best-known independent online forum, however, is Indonesia-l, which is a reliable source of information, as well as providing a new outlet for the printed media.

The government's readiness to imprison journalists like Ahmad Taufik and Eko Maryadi of *Independen* magazine (*Index* 5/1995) showed that they will not tolerate an independent press. Yet the threats don't work: there are currently more than 300 unlicensed magazines and tabloids being published by student activists. And, when *Independen* was banned in March 1995, a new magazine, *Suara Independen* (Independent Voice), took its place.

A renewed wave of repression in October last year resulted in a police raid on the printing house handling *Suara Independen*. The printing house manager, Andi Syahputra, is currently facing up to seven years in jail for 'spreading hatred against the government', just for printing the magazine. The government's warning to printers is clear: don't accept any business from the alternative press.

The fight against censorship will not die because of tightening repression, however. Whenever anyone accesses the Internet, prints material and shares it among their friends, circulation is taking place, despite the authorities' attempts to prevent it. *Suara Independen* now appears on Indonesia-l and various NGOs, like Pijar Indonesia which runs KdPnet, use it as a platform for discussion. There are many paths, and many people prepared to take the risk of making truth available.

● ● ● ● ● ● ● ● ● ● ● ● ● ● ● ● ● ● ● ● ● ● ● ● ● ● ● ● ● ● ● ● ●

## GOENAWAN MOHAMAD

# Confront the might

**The instinct to censor is a powerful one — it is also an acknowledgement of the unpredictable power of words**

IN Indonesia censorship has become a ritual of saying 'no' to expressions of difference. A staggering 2,000 books have been banned in Indonesia over the last 30 years, theatrical performances have to go through no less than nine government offices before they get their stage permits. Like many kinds of ritual, the censorship can be brutal and at the same time empty — so empty that it is sometimes only partially observed. To see censorship as a ritual, however, is not to say it is inconsequential. Especially when one considers that censorship can grip you not merely from the office of watchful military officers or zealous bureaucrats, but from somewhere else, from something not far away from your first sentence.

From an early age I knew what it meant to be afraid of words. Probably 'to be afraid of words' is not the right formulation: what really disturbs people is their own inability to control the impact of their words. When I was little I heard people with their nets, lines and hooks say that they would not utter the word 'fish' as long as they were at sea. People going to the forest to cut teak would not use the word 'tiger', but would refer to the animal by another name in order not to invoke the anger of the king of the jungle.

Today people talk about the need to celebrate differences, but I notice that the predominant tenor in the idea of 'multiculturalism' is to use the

GOENAWAN MOHAMAD

word 'culture' as a synonym for 'community' and a euphemism for 'race'.
In other words, an impermeable human unit, complete with its unshifting
centre and clear-cut margins. What follows from this temptation of
difference can be something that runs counter to the need for tolerance.
At the end of the day, what you have may be an apartheid of values. I say
this as a cautionary note, especially when you deal with the question of
freedom of expression, which entails more than just a public space in
which to differ. To me, and I beg you to forgive my bias, the issue of
freedom of expression is not about certain collective precepts and
principles, or the formulation of common values but, like other issues
related to human rights, in the beginning it is about violence and
suffering. The issue starts from a certain sensibility. To quote Emmanuel
Levinas, the French philosopher, it is a sensibility that takes place 'on the
surface of the skin, at the end of the nerve'. In other words, it is a
sensibility when one looks at the face of the victim.

There is a story I love to use as a case in point in which the issue of
freedom is tightly caught up not with a reading of western canons, but
with real murder and real fear. In June 1994 *Tempo* — the magazine I
edited — was banned by the government together with two other
magazines, *Editor* and *DeTik*. Thirty days later, I went to a remote village
on the island of Madura, in the east of Java, more than 1,000 kilometres
from *Tempo*'s office. I was invited to take part in a public 'prayer of
concern', organised by a 100-year-old religious school in the village.
Some 2,000 people attended, including about 50 ulamas. I used to think
that such an expression of sympathy — in this case for *Tempo*, an urban-
based publication — would only take place on campuses or among the
middle classes. So I asked the host why, of all people, he did it. The
answer was forthright: two months before the banning, four peasants from
the neighbouring village had been shot dead by the military when they
staged a protest against the construction of a dam on their land. *Tempo* and
others sent reporters to cover the incident and, when the story was
published, it attracted nationwide attention and the central government
was forced to act to appease the anger of the Madurese. By having
independent press coverage to publicise their plight, the Madurese had
found some kind of protection. Their fear was that, with a press that
could no longer work freely, more murders could take place unnoticed,
more abuses unchecked. Whoever says that when freedom dies it never
dies alone is absolutely right.

The Madurese episode persuaded me to believe that there has always been a social history of horror, or at least anxiety, in the background of freedom and the absence of it.

In the beginning, in a time when man had a limited technology of survival and when social relations were created by traumas of repression and shared poverty, words were treated almost like a *keris*, the traditional dagger: at times an emblem of ceremony but, nonetheless, forever containing the possibility of harm. Because words can so easily incite aggression and conflict, like the *keris* they are more often than not left silent inside their sheath.

● ● ● ● ● ● ● ● ● ● ● ● ● ● ● ● ● ● ● ● ● ● ● ● ● ● ● ● ● ● ●

**Power, while seeming to fuse with words through the process of their multiplication and distribution, eventually causes words themselves to become unfree**

● ● ● ● ● ● ● ● ● ● ● ● ● ● ● ● ● ● ● ● ● ● ● ● ● ● ● ● ● ● ●

Later, when words entered the era of printing, the anxiety about what they would bring about, and the lack of freedom resulting from that anxiety, became even greater.

In many ancient literary works, which were written in manuscript form and read aloud before a limited and intimate audience, writers could discuss God and sex without much inhibition. In the *Serat Centini*, for instance, an eighteenth-century Javanese poetic text in several volumes, erotic passages describe what is generally found in male sexual fantasy: the endless desire for a woman's body and even a homosexual episode between a local bigshot and a male dancer.

The world of a manuscript text was a world more or less shaped by proximity to an unfragmented community of listeners. In that familiar space, we are able to speak to an audience with whom we immediately share values and metaphors. But then capital and print technology arrived, and there were no more works like the *Centini*. Writers — who since that time, moreover, could no longer be concealed by anonymity — became more cautious in expressing what they experienced in dreams and in daily life, especially concerning God and sex. They no longer had direct acquaintance with the readership for whom they composed literature. They entered a world easily shocked, suspicious, uncomprehending or angry about what they had to say. Perhaps that is really the paradox of words in an age when printing and book publishing are expanding rapidly. Power, while seeming to fuse with words through the process of their multiplication and distribution, eventually causes words themselves to become unfree.

During the 1940s, when modern Indonesian literature was mainly circulated among a small circle of literati, there came to the fore an amazing poet called Chairil Anwar. He not only wrote lyrical and moving poems, he wrote about things that had never been written before. His creative period was that of Indonesia's recent independence from the Netherlands, a time when hopes, like fireworks, were displayed to celebrate the dream of a free country. Chairil Anwar's poetry was fresh and insolent. 'Aku suka pada mereka yang berani hidup' (I prefer those who dare to live), he said, and 'Aku suka pada mereka yang masuk menemu malam' (I prefer those who enter and confront the night). For Chairil it was of no concern that the night held danger, sin, blasphemy or demons. For him there was no fear, no administrative sanction, no religious doctrine, no censor, nor any other limiting factor.

One of his poems speaks of heaven in a satirical tone using imagery popular among Indonesian Muslims:

*Bersungai susu   dan bertabur bidadari beribu*
Complete with a river of milk   and stocked with thousands of nymphs

The poet asks whether among those nymphs there are any as arousing as the young girls on earth. In other words, his attitude celebrates this life more than it does the next. In another poem, 'Di Mesjid', he portrays an encounter with God as a kind of conflict:

*Ini ruang   Gelanggang kami berperang*
This space is   the arena in which we battle each other

Chairil Anwar died young, before the 1940s ended. In the history of Indonesian literature, his was the first and the last insolence. Twenty years later the editor of a literary journal was sentenced — though not jailed, as the sentence was suspended — following a loud protest concerning a short story. The editor, H B Jassin, published in the magazine *Sastra* an allegory about the degenerate morals of the times, in which God was pictured wearing golden eyeglasses, sending the prophet Mohammed, disguised as a bird, to witness the present destruction on earth. A number of religious leaders were angered by the story, and a group of youths broke up *Sastra*'s office. They considered that story, 'Langit Makin Mendung' (The Sky is Getting Darker), offensive to God.

That was in 1968. Times had changed. Or, the times once again confirmed the feeling of fear and vigilance, in a new form, toward those who produce words, as though the potential for violating sacred norms were inherent within them. Today, no writer in Indonesia would dare to provoke such a feeling of fear and vigilance. He or she may even have internalised the need to be censored. In short, many things have happened since Chairil Anwar fought with God in the mosque. Yet somehow, stories and poetry have become too much a part of our lives. In its finest manifestations, literature once again shows us how words can do unexpected things, can explore uncharted territory, leaving only footprints that mock every kind of fettering. And thus it proves how empty is the ritual of censorship, and how difficult for anyone to submit to it forever. ❏

*Goenawan Mohamad was editor-in-chief of* Tempo *magazine until its banning in June 1994. He now heads the Institute for the Studies on Free Flow of Information (ISAI) and is chairman of the Independent Committee for Monitoring the Elections (KIPP). This article is based on his opening speech at the PEN Congress in October 1995*

● ● ● ● ● ● ● ● ● ● ● ● ● ● ● ● ● ● ● ● ● ● ● ● ● ● ● ● ● ●

# WIJI THUKUL

# This dark night

*A*ward-winning poet Wiji Thukul is currently in hiding and being sought by the police in connection with the Jakarta riots of 27 July 1996. Thukul, who chairs the People's Art Network (an organisation under the umbrella of the People's Democratic Party), left school at the age of 11 and took a variety of jobs, including selling newspapers, working as a carpenter, and as a pedicab driver, while composing his poetry. His books include Mencari Tanah Lapang (Looking for Open Fields), Puisi Pelo (A Lisper's Poetry), Darman dan Lain-Lain (Darman and Others). This poem was written while in hiding

(Untitled)

tonight the rain falls
to protect me

those poorly paid intelligence guys
are fed up with their boss for sure

tonight the rain falls
to protect me

so I can rest
so my energy can be restored
after days of exhaustion
so I can stay fresh
and win

tonight the rain falls
to protect me

the croaking of frogs and the whistling
wind
make my eyelids heavy

i'm tired and want to sleep

let the soldiers in the capital
stand guard with their M16s

let the masters be occupied
with their own fears

because they've already
planted
time bombs everywhere

they create enemies
and then shoot them

they create riots
and then break them up

tonight the rain falls
to protect me

this dark night is for me
this dark night is my blanket

sleep well my country
sleep well my wife and kids
the moment will come
will come for freedom
for everyone

11 August 1996

## PRAMOEDYA ANANTA TOER

# 'I can only oppose with words'

The name of Indonesia's most frequently banned writer,
Pramoedya Ananta Toer, crops up in the media each year in the
run-up to Hari Kesaktian Pancasila (Pancasila Victory Day) on
1 October, the national celebration of the defeat of
Communism in 1965. So too does the accusation that he was
involved in the censorship and oppression of writers by the PKI
in the early 1960s. Pramoedya is held up as a warning that the
Communist threat lives on, as a scapegoat that people can
denigrate and condemn with impunity. He has recently been
interrogated in the subversion cases brought against members
of the People's Democratic Party (PRD) in connection with the
Jakarta riots

WHEN a book of mine is banned it's like getting a badge of honour pinned on my chest, because each banning gets wide publicity in the international community. The more they are banned, the more response there is from the democratic world, so the banning of books is not a problem for me.

The powers that be are truly frightened to grow up. If the reasons they give for banning books are just, then why don't they ban them openly through the courts? It's easy enough, much more so than banning without due process and then being criticised throughout the world. The real problem is that the legal system in Indonesia doesn't work. If the authorities were adult about things then they would try to understand the situation. But they don't. They just want to show how powerful they are, even if that means killing people. What can we expect from a government like that? That's why I urge all my friends to uphold human rights themselves. The authorities here don't guarantee respect for human rights.

Bannings make no contribution to Indonesia's development. Whereas writing a book can take years, banning one takes a mere five minutes. Books by their very nature are the property of the public, not of the people who ban them. If a writer feels that what he is doing is right, he should go ahead and write.

When I was in prison on Buru Island I only had two practical problems: coping with prison officials and with friends who liked to disturb me. That's all. On Buru I had to fend for myself to get food to eat. But fortunately I had several friends there who were happy to work in my place, which gave me the opportunity to write almost full time, except for the mornings when I had to cut wood for the kitchen stove.

For reference material I had to rely entirely on memory. As it happened, when I was young I had often read *Babad Tanah Jawa* [the Chronicle of Java] in various versions, including that of my parents. And as a teenager I read a lot of western books. So that helped.

Nowadays in Indonesia there are writers who are in the pocket of the authorities and there are those who are outside of that world. Those who are in the pockets of the authorities mainly busy themselves with producing light material aimed at helping people forget the reality around them. The more repressive the situation, the more entertainment will develop to provide an escape from reality. I don't concern myself with those who are in the pockets of the power-holders. As far as I'm concerned they don't exist. Their work is simply to glorify their masters.

• • • • • • • • • • • • • • • • • • • • • • • • • • • • • •

# Letter to my daughter

**S**ince 14 November 1973 I've not had to work in the fields, which means, for all practical purposes, that I've not been working for my own food. I survive from the sweat of my friends. It is they who provide me with food and drink. The only thing I have to get for myself is my bath water. My normal food ration is three plates of rice a day plus some greens, but my mates don't leave it at that. They always try to make sure I get something extra, and even help to keep me supplied with cigarettes, clothing, sugar and soap. Each month they give me two reams of onionskin paper, a typing ribbon and carbon paper, and when my rickety old typewriter finally broke, they rushed to fix it for me. When I'm sick they take care of me. They love me, Tieknong, and I love them. I shall never forget their kindness. They travel a good distance to see me, as far away as 10 kilometres, carrying bananas or papayas or fish for me. I know that I can't repay their kindness individually but I swear that someday I'll find a way to make it up to them, even if they themselves have given no thought to recompense at all.

In the 12 years that I've been here I've met so many, so very many, good-hearted people. They help me to remember the things I have forgotten. They air their complaints to me and ask me for advice on dealing with family problems. I feel now that their families are my family, too. As the days pass, more and more of them die,

The awards I have won confirm that all this time I have been in the right. Of course they make me very happy. Especially since I've been denigrated over and over again throughout the New Order period. These awards give me strength, especially the one I got last year from the PRD.

From the moment I was called for interrogation as a witness in the PRD cases I knew what was going to happen. Right from the beginning, before any arrests had been made, everyone, even the president himself, was bad-mouthing the PRD. This young people's organisation was regarded as having been responsible for the 27 July riots. The prosecutor said that I was pro-PRD. If the president declares the PRD to have done wrong before the trials even start, what can the trial officials do? I cannot far from sight of the people they love and the people who love them. And there they are, by themselves, alone and silent in untended graves on the mountainside and in the arid plain. A wooden post, a makeshift gravestone, with their date of birth and death, is all that marks their graves. Most of those who have died are younger than your father. And sometimes, after they're dead, a long-awaited letter arrives from home — two, four, even five years late. Such things as this make me cry. Two months ago one of my mates, a man by the name of Mulyoso, a graduate of the Jember Sports Training Academy, had his head split open with a hoe handle. The man who killed him was Bahsan, a young man from Jakarta, only 27 years of age who had been 16 years old when he was brought here! A few days after Mulyoso was buried a package from his mother and family in Semarang arrived, one the deceased had been waiting for for 12 years.

These past 12 years have been a period of intense hardship for me. So many of my friends are now dead. Life is to be devoted to the continued safety and prosperity of mankind. And, as Buddha taught, suffering is always the result of stupidity and ignorance.

*Excerpted from chapter 11 of* Nyanyi Sunyii Seorang Bisu II, *'Belated birthday gift for my Tieknong on her 21st birthday' (Lentera, Jakarta, February 1997); to be published in English in 1998 under the title* The Mute's Soliloquy
*© Translation Willem Samuels*

● ● ● ● ● ● ● ● ● ● ● ● ● ● ● ● ● ● ● ● ● ● ● ● ● ● ● ● ● ● ●

fathom how any Indonesian can behave like this.

I still want to write. But I can't work somewhere as noisy as this. I really need to go to the countryside, but the problem is that my security cannot be guaranteed there. If I go out of town, I have to do so quietly, without anyone being aware of the fact. That's the only way I feel safe. After all, I can only oppose with words. Basically, if I am harassed, I respond. I'm old, what else can I do? ❏

*Interviewed by Stanley*

## PARNO PARIKENO

# Puppets and masters

**Theatre cannot bring a government down — at least so theatre people and theatre-goers believe. The bureaucracy and security forces apparently think otherwise**

CENSORSHIP and banning in the arts is not part of a coherent policy of culture-building by the government. The New Order could be said to be indifferent to literature, theatre, fine arts and modern music: modern art attracting small audiences, that is, as opposed to traditional arts such as *wayang kulit* (shadow puppetry). The authorities only get interested if a play or a poetry reading, for example, draws big audiences and gets wide coverage in the media.

Take the case of the company Teater Koma. Since 1977 they have produced plays which are accessible, witty and full of social comment. In Jakarta their performances can attract 16,000 people or more, perhaps the largest such audiences in southeast Asia. In 1990, however, the police stopped the Jakarta run of their play *Suksesi* (Succession) after 11 days (it had been due to run for 14). The only explanation came the day after the ban: *Suksesi* was deemed 'not educational' and 'could cause unexpected things to happen'. No explicit reason was given regarding the play's content. Maybe the real reason was that it was a parody on the handover of political power, or that it was a satire on President Suharto's children and their business concerns? That was what many people suspected.

Other companies have run into trouble because their material bears a close relationship to actual events. The play *Pak Kanjeng* concerns a veteran of the war of independence who loses his land three times: once to a factory, then to a dam and finally to a golf course. In 1993 it was performed without incident in Yogyakarta by a theatre group which included the well-known social critic and poet Emha Ainan Nadjib, but the following year in Surabaya it was banned. As far as the regional military authorities were concerned, the play alluded to the Nipah incident in Madura, in which four people were shot dead while protesting the building of a dam on their land. The same year the poet Darmanto Jatman was banned from reading one of his poems, entitled 'Golf untuk rakyat' (Golf for the people) in Yogyakarta, because a golf course was in the process of being built nearby.

If modern theatre gets only sporadic attention, it is a very different matter for the traditional art form which these days is becoming ever more popular among Javanese, namely *wayang kulit* (shadow puppetry). *Wayang kulit*, which often uses stories from the Mahabharata and the Ramayana, is also popular among Javanese government officials of all ranks. In 1994 dozens of *dalang* (puppet masters) and artists from other styles of traditional theatre were invited to Wonogiri, Central Java, and informed about the nuclear electricity generating plant due to be built in Jepara. It is well known that this project has encountered strong opposition from local leaders, environmentalists and NGOs.

Nowadays it is also common for officials to use puppet masters to spread the government's views on development. As a result *wayang kulit* performances often contain advice about the importance of transmigration, family planning, the general elections and so on. The ruling party, Golkar, often holds parties where they put on *wayang kulit* performances using famous puppet masters. But then, as one puppet master commented, puppet masters have been used as the mouthpiece of the authorities since the sixteenth century. Another very popular puppet master defended this on the grounds that it is better to be a mouthpiece of the government than a mouthpiece for revolt.

In 1995 President Suharto, a great lover of *wayang kulit*, suggested that puppet masters perform the play *Semar Mbabar Jati Diri* (Semar Seeks his Identity). Semar is a Javanese leader not found in the Indian Mahabharata or Ramayana. He is like a wise clown, a god who is cursed to become an ordinary man, who becomes the servant and adviser to five brothers, good noblemen of the Pandawa family. The government has always sought to identify itself with Pandawa, so *Semar Mbabar Jati Diri* was intended as a way of promoting the ordinary man, rather than the nobility who are all too often the focus of *wayang kulit* performances. The puppet masters who were gathered together in order to write the play came up with a work that is truly mystical and, more importantly, is free of any reference to social realities. In it Semar becomes a mediator between the descendants of two noblemen — Pandawa and Kurawa — who quarrel. Semar's overriding message is the need to maintain harmony and tradition — clearly in line with the government's 'stability and security' policy.

Until it was outlawed and destroyed in September 1965, the Indonesian Communist Party (PKI) also used shadow puppetry as a propaganda tool. Nowadays the New Order government is clearly serious about using shadow puppetry as its mouthpiece. Indeed shadow puppet performances in Javanese are a very powerful means of communication: a large percentage of Javanese people only use the national language, Bahasa Indonesia, as their second language. At the same time, for some puppet masters aligning themselves with the government means security, not being regarded with suspicion for having a large following, as well as ensuring plenty of commissions. All in all, it provides a way of forgetting the political trauma of the PKI period.

What is happening in the theatre is only one of the actions being taken by a paranoid government. What are they afraid of? Of intellectuals and the middle classes who enjoy modern art? Sure, criticism can emerge from the theatre in the same way as it can from a scientific experiment carried out in a laboratory. And it is only right and proper for theatre to be a venue for countering the official jargon and rigidity of thought. Theatre has never proved to be a cause of disturbances or riots. On the contrary, it is the censors themselves who are the source of suspicion and hatred.

Meanwhile, the popularity of *wayang kulit* works in tandem with the notions of origin, indigenousness, nationality and eastern values proclaimed by the New Order. New interpretations of *wayang* stories are becoming fewer or have ceased, a consequence of the traditionalism which parallels the reluctance of the New Order to accept any change to the status quo. That is why democracy and openness cannot be expected from the New Order, but must rather be sought by the people themselves. Whether artists spoil or enlighten their public, a public which is already full of sermons on development, depends on the ability of those artists to overcome their own feelings of fear. ❑

*Parno Parikeno is a writer and essayist based in Jakarta*

## SOPHAN SOPHIAAN

# Death by a thousand cuts

*The star of 50 films and director of 18 more, Sophan Sophiaan knows Indonesia's censorship system from the inside. Now a member of parliament, he continues to speak out on behalf of what remains of the film industry*

The censorship process begins with the first script, most of whose contents are scratched out and amended. Then the script is returned. And so it goes on, back and forth, until the final product becomes celluloid — and then it's censored again so it can be distributed. In my own case, I sometimes wondered whether the final product was really my own film. The Board of Film Censorship have criteria on sex and sadism, for example, which you're not supposed to show on film, but they often let such things through. If a film contains some social realism on the other hand, it's immediately cut. I don't know whether this is just a matter of the individual censor's taste or an order from above.

Producers and script writers know that films that reflect social realities are going to be cut so they practise a lot of self-censorship. Over the years that pressure builds up, with the result that many of our directors — including me — have lost their creativity. I haven't made a film for five years. I once planned to make a film about a doctor who falls in love with his nurse. It wasn't allowed because it was 'unsuitable'. It was cut. Another time I wanted to make a film about the pioneering career of a diplomat, an Indonesian ambassador, but that wasn't allowed because I had to get permission from Bakin [the national intelligence agency]. The Department of Foreign Affairs says that its ambassadors are state officials and, as such, may not be 'belittled' by being portrayed in a film.

So the number of films being produced goes down, to the point where I no longer think the industry can be revived. It's already in such a bad state — there isn't even a film festival any more, because there really aren't any films worth celebrating. In the end, film-goers become apathetic about Indonesian films, and it's very hard to change their opinions because they have only ever seen bad Indonesian films. They think that an Indonesian film must be bad by definition. And so American films become easier to distribute in Indonesia. *Interview by Gedsiri Suhartono*

● ● ● ● ● ● ● ● ● ● ● ● ● ● ● ● ● ● ● ● ● ● ● ● ● ● ● ● ● ● ●

# IWAN FALS

# Guitar versus tanks

IDH

*Known as 'the Indonesian Bob Dylan', Iwan Fals is one of the country's most popular singers. Many of his ballads address important social and political matters. He has repeatedly been approached by both opposition parties to stand for Parliament, but says he is not interested. His live performances are frequently banned. In 1984 the army halted a show in Pekanbaru, Sumatra, on the grounds that two of his songs — 'Demokrasi Nasi' (Rice Democracy) and 'Mbak Tini' (Sister Tini) — were a threat to public order. In 1989 the police banned his 100-town tour. 'All I carry is a guitar made of wood and strings,' he said then. 'How can this be dangerous, compared to a tank?' And his shows continue to be banned — most recently in Ujung Pandang in 1996*

I've never been given a clear reason for the bans. It's a question I ask the promoters again and again. When the authorities get an application for permission to stage a concert, they just say 'next time, yeah?' But they've never given me a clear reason why. I don't know why they don't just say 'Iwan, you're banned!' and be done with it.

I don't have any plans to perform at the moment. Apparently several promoters are considering the idea in the context of what's going on now — with the elections coming up, the riots in Situbondo, Tasikmalaya and so on. I'm quite concerned too. If something happens that they say is 'subversive' or something like that, it could have an impact on my whole life. So in the end I've decided it's best just to be silent. But if a promoter asks me to perform, I won't be able to refuse.

In the end, freedom, or the lack of freedom, depends on the individual. The creative process is inside. But of course if you want to put on a show then that depends on the situation around you. If that isn't free then that will have an effect. Political factors do impose limits and, if they are to the detriment of public artistic expression, then that must be opposed. How? Just by talking. By saying: 'This isn't right.' How can we create without an audience?

*Interviewed by Binyo*

'Hooray — riots'

What happens if mouths are banned from speaking?
What happens if eyes are banned from seeing?
What happens if ears are banned from hearing?
We become robots without souls
Which only obey orders

What happens if suggestions become threats?
What happens if moneylenders squeeze the people?
What happens if greed becomes uncontrollable?
We get injustice
Which only gives rise to revenge

[Refrain ......]

What happens if farmers lose their land?
What happens if brokers control all the land?
What happens if law is a symbol just for show?
You get exploitation of some by others
Which only gives rise to Draculas

*Iwan Fals and Sawung Jabo*

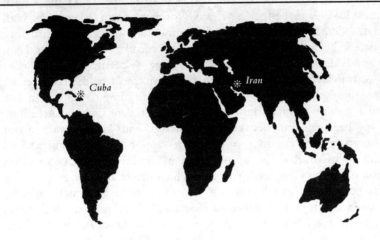

## No news is good news

As THIS issue goes to press, the US-based Cable News Network (CNN) is about to open a bureau in Havana, bringing to an end 28 years of non-co-operation between Cuba and the USA in the field of news provision. Since 1969, when the Associated Press was pushed out of Cuba, there has been no permanent US news presence on the island. CNN's deal changes all that.

It doesn't signal any warming in the cold-war attitudes that still govern US-Cuban relations, however. CNN is the beneficiary of a special set of circumstances: the personal friendship between its founder, Ted Turner, and President Castro; and Washington's desire to put the Cuban government on the defensive by challenging them to accept a US news organisation on the ground. That desire also underlies Washington's decision to give permission to nine other US news organisations to set up in Cuba: it's great propaganda to put Castro in the position of denying access to the 'free Western press'. It's interesting to speculate whether the US will in turn give the go-ahead for Cuba's state-run press agency Prensa Latina, or the Communist Party daily *Granma* to open bureaux in Washington.

What gets overlooked in all the fun and games, though, is the fact that Cuba itself has a thriving independent indigenous press. True, it's poorly funded, it operates beyond the margins of the law, and its lack of resources is reflected in the quality of its output, when compared with either Cuba's state media or America's vast media corporations. In recent weeks the Cuban authorities have launched a new wave of harassment against it, with orchestrated demonstrations outside the homes of independent journalists, summary searches and arbitrary arrests. That people like Néstor Baguer, Raul Rivero and Rafaela Lasalle — to name but three — persist with their work regardless, is evidence of an extraordinary commitment to the task. Yet it's hard to see how the presence of a CNN bureau is going to help them one bit in their attempt to carve out a space for independent Cuban journalism.

The propaganda war between Washington and Havana isn't about Communism or press freedom, of course, it's about dollars. Specifically, it's about the Helms-Burton law, an unprecedentedly broad piece of sanctions legislation passed by Congress a year ago, which makes any foreign company liable for prosecution in US courts if they profit from investments in US-owned assets or property confiscated after the 1959 Cuban revolution. It's convenient for the US government to pretend that the sanctions are meant to promote democracy and human rights in Cuba. In reality they are designed to protect commercial interests.

It's the same with that other American foreign policy *bête noire*, Iran. Under the Iran-Libya Sanctions Act passed last August, foreign oil companies can be penalised if they invest more than US$40 million in Iran's oil or gas industries. In a rare admission at the end of January, one senior Iranian politician acknowledged that the sanctions have bitten. 'Foreign contractors aren't much interested in engaging in petroleum projects in Iran,' said Mohsen Yahyavi of the parliamentary oil commission. Yet the human rights situation in Iran only gets worse.

The bizarre and horrifying case of *Adineh* editor Faraj Sarkoohi has focused attention on the suffering of all writers and intellectuals in the current climate in Iran. Sarkoohi's own account of his detention, torture, slander and humiliation at the hands of the security services, is detailed in a harrowing letter written during a brief period of freedom in early January (see page 90). But he is far from the only victim of his country's turn toward extremism. With the Rafsanjani government apparently losing its grip and the forces of revolutionary theocracy threatening to regain the upper hand, no-one is safe. And neither the US policy of isolation, nor the European Union's policy of 'critical dialogue' is able to turn that tide. ❏

*Adam Newey*

*A censorship chronicle incorporating information from the American Association for the Advancement of Science Human Rights Action Network (AAASHRAN), Amnesty International (AI), Article 19 (A19), the BBC Monitoring Service Summary of World Broadcasts (SWB), the Committee to Protect Journalists (CPJ), the Inter-American Press Association (IAPA), the International Federation of Journalists (IFJ/FIP), Human Rights Watch (HRW), the Media Institute of Southern Africa (MISA), the Network for the Defence of Independent Media in Africa (NDIMA), International PEN (PEN), the Open Media Research Institute (OMRI), Reporters Sans Frontières (RSF), the World Association of Community Broadcasters (AMARC), the World Organisation Against Torture (OMCT) and other sources*

## AFGHANISTAN

The Taliban Islamic militia, which currently controls more than two-thirds of the country, has said that it will soon lift its ban on television, but will allow only broadcasts that conform to Islamic law. **Shafiqa Habibi**, the longest-serving announcer on state television and radio and one of the most famous faces in Afghanistan prior to the Taliban takeover, has disappeared from public view. She has been engaged in talks with Taliban officials in the hope of winning a return to the workplace for 300 female staff members of Radio Afghanistan (renamed Radio Sharia). (*Guardian*)

## ALBANIA

**Roland Beqiraj**, a correspondent for *Koha Jone*, was detained and beaten by police in Korca on 26 January. It is believed that Beqiraj was detained because of an article entitled 'Protesters Burn Portrait of President Sali Berisha', describing the riots sparked by the collapse of pyramid investment schemes. The authorities accused him of taking part in the demonstrations. He was released on 7 February. (SWB)

On 1 February *Koha Jone* correspondent **Anilda Ibrahami** was expelled from a meeting of the ruling Democratic Party in Vlora following vocal criticism of the paper. On 5 February a truck carrying copies of *Koha Jone* to Vlora where demonstrations were due to take place was blocked and forbidden to enter the town. On 4 and 5 February blank spaces appeared in *Koha Jone* where government censors had cut articles. Genc Cobani, associate editor-in-chief of the daily *Republika*, was interrogated about his presence in Vlora on 15 February by several men thought to be members of the secret police. The men beat him so badly that he required hospital treatment. (CPJ, RSF)

Several assaults on journalists were reported on 8 February. In Tirana **Leon Cika**, a Reuters cameraman was struck by police and **Arben Celi**, a photographer for Reuters, had his equipment taken. Also, three members of the security police attempted to seize video footage of the demonstrations from the Reuters offices. In Fier, **Benet Koleka**, a Reuters journalist, was beaten by police and his notebook was confiscated. **Spiro Ilo**, a cameraman, and **Hektor Pustina**, a photojournalist, both with Associated Press, were also beaten by plainclothes police. **Ben Blushi**, editor-in-chief of *Koha Jone* was threatened in front of his house and **Prec Zogaj**, editor-in-chief of the daily *Dita Informacion*, was beaten by secret police in Tirana. Other journalists reportedly ill-treated are Vladimir Gozhi, Arben Gega, Stavri Shkembi, Gjergji Meta, Ermir Caci and B Memushi. (RSF, IFJ, AI)

## ALGERIA

Publication of the independent French-language daily *La Tribune* resumed on 11 February, seven months after it was banned for publishing a cartoon deemed offensive to the national flag (*Index* 5/1996). (IFJ)

Journalist **Khaled Aboulkacem**, researcher for the French-language paper *L'Indépendant*, was attacked by suspected Islamist gunmen and shot dead on 13 January as he was leaving the newspaper's offices in Algiers. **Nourredine Guittoune**, the paper's owner, manager and editor-in-chief, was wounded in the shoulder and abdomen in the attack. (IFJ)

The government has announced that it wants Arabic to have replaced the French language for most official functions and in teaching by the year 2000, effectively making the language compulsory in public life and ending the official use of other languages almost immediately. Officials who use French or English in statements or documents could be fined up to 10,000 dinars (US$175) for infringing the new law. (*Jane's Intelligence Review*)

The government-appointed Transitional National Council approved a law on 18 February that bans political parties from having a political platform based on Islam. The law gives two legal Islamist parties, Nahda and Hamas, two months to change their manifestos to avoid running foul of the legislation. (Reuters)

## ARGENTINA

A photographer for *Noticias* magazine was found murdered in a burnt-out car near the beach resort of Pinamar, southeast of Buenos Aires on 25 January. **José Luis Cabezas** had been handcuffed, set alight and shot in the head. A highly regarded photographer, he had been sent to Pinamar to seek pictures of holidaying government officials and top businessmen. President Menem has played down suggestions that Cabezas was killed for political reasons. The independent journalists' rights group Periodistas condemned it as 'a very serious event that is all too reminiscent of similar incidents not so long ago in Argentina's history.' (CPJ, Reuters, *Latinamerica Press*)

**Santo Biasatti**, a well-known radio and TV journalist, has been receiving anonymous death threats against himself and members of his family. On 7 February an anonymous caller left a telephone message for him saying that 'he would suffer the same fate as Cabezas'. This was followed by warnings that 'the one who will suffer most is his granddaughter'. On 8 and 9 February messages were left alleging that provincial policemen would be carrying out a contract to abduct Biasatti. (AI)

## ARMENIA

**Artush Hamazaspyan**, a local leader of the opposition National Self-Determination Union (AIM), is still under arrest on charges of 'participation in mass disorder' in the wake of the 25 September 1996 post-election unrest in Yerevan. He is reported to have been badly beaten while in custody. Out of 27 AIM members arrested after the elections, Hamazaspyan is the only one still in custody. Meanwhile, the US government has urged prime minister Armen Sarkisyan, who visited Washington in early January, to hold fresh parliamentary elections. (OMRI)

## AUSTRALIA

On 10 January Olympic Games minister Michael Knight confirmed that would-be house buyers within the Olympic 2000 precinct, Homebush, will be thoroughly screened. Residents and businesses will

have to agree to ongoing checks including security patrols and restrictions on advertising. The Privacy Commission has expressed concern about the distribution of information about residents leading up to and after the games. (Reuters)

Broadcasters must impose stricter self-regulation if they are to avoid enforced restrictions in an increasingly conservative climate, according to a report published in February. In its first review since self-regulation was introduced in 1993, the Federation of Australian Commercial Television Stations proposed a new classification, AV (Adult Violence), for programmes deemed too violent for the current MA (Mature Audience) rating. The AV programmes will be screen at 9.30pm, half an hour later than MA-rated programmes. (Reuters)

## BAHRAIN

On 16 February **Ali Hassan Yousif**, a writer and poet, was arrested after his house was raided by members of the intelligence department. No reason has been given for the arrest but a few weeks earlier Yousif was dismissed from his post at the Ministry of Information and his book *Isharat* (Symbols) was banned. In *Isharat* Yousif describes his views on oppression, without specifically talking about Bahrain. (Bahrain Human Rights Organisation, PEN)

On 20 February the information minister issued an order

aimed at restricting the work of foreign journalists and reporters in Bahrain. All correspondents for foreign news organisations are required to renew their accreditation annually, and cannot claim diplomatic immunity. At the end of January the minister submitted a formal complaint against Agence France-Presse (AFP) for its coverage of events in Bahrain. (Bahrain Freedom Movement)

## BANGLADESH

Police arrested the headmaster and a teacher of a school in Chittagong on 10 December for keeping 21 students in chains and starving them for three days. They were being punished for failing to study. (*Times*)

The Appeal Court dismissed an application by the writer **Taslima Nasrin** (*Index* 2/1995, 10/1993) for leave to appeal against her prosecution on 17 February. The case must now be dealt with by the trial court. (A19)

## BELARUS

President Alaksander Lukashenka announced that a second state television channel will broadcast on the frequency until now used by **Russian Public TV (ORT)** on 13 January. ORT is the most popular TV channel in Belarus but Lukashenka is unhappy with its criticism of him. On 15 January it was announced that the frequency used by the independent radio station **101.2 FM**, which was banned in September 1996, has been

reallocated to a new state-run youth station. (OMRI, RSF, SWB)

Poet and columnist **Slavamir Adamovich** (*Index* 1/1997) was released on 7 February. Charges relating to his poem 'Kill the President' were dropped. (PEN)

On 11 February Vladimir Pavlovitch, head of the media division of the President's Office, informed Aleksandr Stupnikov, Minsk correspondent for the Russian station **NTV**, of a protest letter sent to Russia's Ministry of External Affairs, criticising the 'subjectivity' of his reporting. It was implied that NTV transmissions could be terminated if 'uncertain news' continued to be broadcast. (RSF)

## BOSNIA-HERCEGOVINA

Representatives of the Catholic Church said on 10 December 1996 that it held Bosnian Television and other Sarajevo media responsible for an attack on two Catholic priests in Sarajevo on 8 December. The assailant reportedly kept shouting 'Now you will see how a Muslim beats' and 'Why do you beat us in Mostar?'. The Church complained that the Sarajevo media accused Croats for everything that happened in Mostar, and helped to foster national hatred. (SWB)

Kosta Jovanovic, the director of Bosnia's internationally funded independent television network TVIN, said on 7 January that broadcasting

would resume after satellite problems had interrupted transmission. During the interruptions, Bosnia's state-run media claimed the station had stopped broadcasting because of a financial scandal. Jovanovic denied the accusations which he described as a deliberate attempt to discredit the network. (OMRI)

Recent publication: *The Unindicted — Reaping the Rewards of 'Ethnic Cleansing'* (HRW/Helsinki, January 1997, 76pp)

## BRAZIL

On 20 December 1996 **Antonio Stelio de Castro**, director-general of the paper *Pagina 20*, was assaulted and his staff threatened with a pistol by Roberto Filho, a deputy for the state of Acre. Filho also threatened to kill **Altino Machado**, correspondent for the Jornal do Brasil news agency. Machado published an article in *Pagina 20* which contained accusations against Filho's wife of complicity in entrance-exam fraud at the Federal University of Acre. (IAPA)

TV Mundial correspondent **Natan Pereira Gatinho** was murdered in Paragominas, Para state, on 11 January, apparently in a contract killing. He had recently told colleagues that he had been receiving death threats. In 1996 he had criticised a poultry company and reported on the appropriation of land in the region by big landowners and on exploitative practices in the state's forestry industry. (RSF)

## BULGARIA

On 11 January at least five journalists were assaulted by police during a mass demonstration outside Parliament held to demand early elections. They included the photojournalists **Velko Angelov** of the weekly *Capital*, **Raly Marinov** of *Zemedelsko Zname*, and freelancer **Assen Tonev**, as well as **Irina Alexieva**, a reporter for the private radio station Darik, and **Sava Dinev**, correspondent for Radio France International. (RSF)

State television journalists protested against censorship of coverage of the demonstrations by displaying notices with the slogans 'Warning, protest action' before and after the main news and by playing the Beatles' song 'Let It Be', which was also used in the anti-Communist protests of 1990. National radio has also been widely criticised for lagging behind private stations in its coverage of events. (Reuters, SWB)

## BURMA

Television, video, and computer-game centres were banned in Rangoon on 16 January on the grounds that they amount to illegal gambling and could damage public morality. (SWB)

On 18 January the SLORC announced that 20 people have been sentenced to seven years' imprisonment for 'inciting and agitating students and non-students' during the December protests in Rangoon (*Index* 1/1997).

Seven of those sentenced were members of Aung San Suu Kyi's National League for Democracy (NLD). (AI)

According to a statement made by Aung San Suu Kyi on 3 February, 105 people are still in detention in connection with the December protests, among them 34 NLD supporters and members. Amnesty International estimates over 2,000 people were detained for their part in human rights protests in Burma in 1996. Public access to Suu Kyi's home continues to be blocked, apparently for her 'personal safety'. (SWB, Reuters)

## CAMBODIA

Nineteen Vietnamese dissidents, believed to be members of the outlawed 'Free Vietnam Movement', were forcibly repatriated on 5 December 1996, in spite of applications for asylum with the UN High Commission for Refugees. On their return, the 19 were detained for investigation pending charges under national security legislation. (AI)

On 2 February the government ordered the municipal authorities in Phnom Penh to close down bars and clubs featuring topless dancers, deemed as a threat to 'good living'. (*Guardian*)

## CAMEROON

**Eyoum Ngangue**, a journalist for the independent daily *Le Messager Popoli*, was arrested in Doula on 22 January following his sentencing to a

year's imprisonment on 3 October last year with editor **Pius Njawe** (*Index* 1/1997) for 'insulting the president and disseminating false information' in an editorial and two cartoons criticising draft constitutional amendments. (AI, RSF)

Recent publication: *Harassment of the Press Continues* (A19, February 1997)

## CHINA

Under pressure from legal reforms which took effect in early 1997, Chinese prosecutors rushed through a series of political prosecutions in December. Those sentenced include **Zhang Zong'ai**, given five years in prison for counter-revolutionary incitement, and democracy activists **Fu Guoyong** (detained since July 1996) and **Chen Ping** (detained since August), charged with publishing counter-revolutionary essays abroad and given three years' education through labour and one year of labour reform respectively (*Index* 6/1996). Others imprisoned were **Li Hai** (detained May 1995), sentenced on 18 December to nine years for prying into state secrets, and **Shen Liangqing** and **Huang Xiuming** (*Index* 1/1997), sentenced to 17 months and one year respectively for counter-revolutionary incitement. **Ma Lianggang**, who stood trial with Shen and Huang, was stripped of his political rights for three years. Under new regulations, the crime of counter-revolution will be replaced by specific statutes on jeopardising state security while administrative detention is to be limited to 30 days. (Reuters, *International Herald Tribune*, Human Rights in China)

More than 20,000 copies of banned books, papers, and periodicals, 200,000 pirated audiovisual discs, and over 300 slot machines, were burnt on the banks of the Hutuo He river in Hebei province on 19 January in the second mass destruction of material in the area. All the items are believed to have been recently impounded in Shijiazhuang. (SWB)

In late January the Propaganda Department published a wide-ranging three-year plan for rectifying newspapers and publications and announced fresh directives for journalists. The regulations, which include the establishment of a hotline for the public to report on journalistic offenders, detail both how news should be written and what it should cover. The practice of 'paid news' is prohibited and reporters are instructed to promote patriotism, respect the Constitution and state and party secrets. Sex, murder, violence, superstition and 'other bad-taste content' are to be avoided and 'the worship of money, hedonism, and individualism' opposed. In addition, a programme of 'investigation and screening' is to be carried out, with special emphasis on internal publications. Internal papers are to be removed from public circulation and prohibited from carrying advertisements. Those that

remain (many were abolished in 1996) are to be given a deadline for improving quality. (SWB, Reuters)

On 22 January China's state news agency, Xinhua, announced a new programme to eliminate cultural decadence and the influence of the West. The Ministry of Culture will curb the building of new nightclubs and video parlours and set an 'appropriate ratio' for the number of imported and domestic programmes available. Piracy and pornography are also to be targeted. Meanwhile, Beijing's Patriotic Public Health Committee has renewed its campaign to discourage smoking in public, with undercover officials inspecting libraries and stations for offenders. (Reuters, *South China Morning Post*)

Journalist **Xi Yang** (*Index* 1&2/1994), Beijing correspondent with daily *Ming Pao*, was freed from prison on 25 January, three years into a 12-year sentence. Xi was found guilty of stealing and publishing state secrets — interest-rate adjustments and plans for international gold transactions by the People's Bank of China. **Tian Ye**, the bank official accused of supplying him with information, continues to serve a 15-year term, handed down at the same time. (CPJ, PEN, SWB, *South China Morning Post*)

*Inner Mongolia*: The original sentences against **Hada** and **Texegi** (*Index* 3/1996) were upheld on 24 January. Held in detention since December

1995, both men were found guilty of separatist activities and espionage on 6 December 1996 and imprisoned for 15 and 10 years respectively. (Reuters, OMCT)

*Xinjiang*: A curfew was imposed on the town of Yining after 10 people died and 198 were injured in separatist rioting in the town on 5-6 February. Conflicting reports suggest that at least 300 people, including alleged ringleader Abudu Heilili, were arrested after the riots, which Uighur separatist groups say were sparked by the execution of some 30 Uighur nationalists arrested in China's 'Strike Hard' anti-crime campaign in 1996. Some sources suggest that 100 Uighurs (including six ringleaders) were subsequently summarily executed for their part in the Yining riots. The town has now been sealed off from the rest of the region. (*Times*, *Guardian*, Reuters, OMRI)

## COLOMBIA

On 16 December 1996 Congress passed a package of constitutional reforms, including measures that place restrictions on press freedom and affect the protection of journalists' sources. Congress also passed a bill which would allow for the revocation and cancellation of television licences. (IAPA)

Two bombs caused extensive damage to newspaper offices at the end of December. The first exploded on 22 December outside the Bogotá offices of the Communist Party weekly *Voz*; the second exploded six days later at the offices of the daily *El Tiempo* in Medellín. (IAPA)

Recent publication: *Hacienda Bellacruz — Land, Violence and Paramilitary Power* (AI, February 1997, 19pp)

## COTE D'IVOIRE

**Freedom Neruda** (*Index* 2/1996, 5/1996, 6/1996), deputy editor of *La Voie*, was released on 1 January. There are unconfirmed reports that **Emmanuel Kore** and **Abou Drahamane Sangare**, detained with Neruda for 'offences to the state', were also released at the same time. (PEN)

On 7 January student activists **Picas Damane, Charles Ble Gouce** and **Sylvanus Gore** were sentenced to two years' imprisonment for 'inciting violence' at a demonstration about scholarship payments on 18 December 1996, despite witness statements that the violence occurred several hours after the rally and was initiated by other people. (AI)

## CROATIA

On 10 December 1996 **Davor Butkovic**, editor-in-chief of the weekly *Globus*, **Vlado Vurusic**, journalist, and **Boris Beribak**, photographer, were sued for libel by the Defence Ministry. The allegations relate to an article claiming that the Bosnian Croat military commander Ivica Rajic, indicted for serious war crimes in Bosnia, was living in the army hotel in Split. The Ministry denied that it was hiding Rajic. (SWB)

On 10 January **Radio 101's** broadcasting licence, due to expire on 15 January, was extended until the end of the month and, on 24 January, a five-year licence was granted. Mass protests in Zagreb frustrated government attempts to close the station in November 1996 (*Index* 1/1997). (SWB, OMRI, *Independent*)

## CUBA

**Rafaela Lasalle**, president and founder of the news agency Oriente Press, was detained in Santiago de Cuba on 7 January by the state security police. The next day one of the agency's journalists, **Daisy Carcaces**, was also detained. No reason has been given for their arrest but local journalists report that they are part of a wider crackdown in the east of the country against political opposition and the independent press. (Independent Press Agency in Cuba)

On 14 January **Nicolas Rosario-Rozabal**, chief correspondent of the Independent Press Agency in Cuba (APIC), was attacked and beaten up by two men in the Santiago de Cuba railway station while waiting for a train to Havana. APIC believes that the beating was carried out by government agents. Rosario-Rozabal was then arrested by police on 23 January having just arrived in Havana by air from Santiago de Cuba. He has been held incommunicado ever since. No reason was given for his arrest. (APIC)

**Juan Francisco Monzon**, president of the Christian Democrat Party, was arrested by police on 26 January. On the same day, **Fernando Sánchez López**, president of the Democratic Solidarity Party (PSD), **Pedro Pablo Alvárez**, president of the United Council of Cuban Workers and other members of the National Co-ordinating Council of Concilio Cubano, were summoned to appear at police headquarters within 12 days. It is not known on what grounds they are to be investigated but these events follow from the arrest of **Héctor Palacio Ruiz**, previous president of the PSD and also a member of Concilio Cubano, on 9 January. He was taken to the Technical Investigations Department (DTI) where he is reportedly being held in a cell without light or ventilation. Unofficial sources say that he is to be tried on a charge of 'disrespect' for allegedly making statements to foreign journalists about declarations made by President Castro at the Sixth Ibero-American Summit in Chile in November 1996. (AI, Habana Press)

The independent news agency Cuba Press has been subjected to a campaign of intimidation by the authorities since mid-January. **Tania Quintero** and **Juan Antonio Sánchez**, reporters with the agency, were arrested outside the Czech embassy in Havana by state security agents on the morning of 21 January. They had just received materials — including a laptop computer — and money donated by a Cuba Press associate in Miami. The money and equipment were confiscated. The two journalists were held incommunicado and interrogated overnight. On 10 February 'acts of repudiation' were held outside the homes of Tania Quintero and **Ana Luis Baeza**, another Cuba Press journalist, during which they were denounced as traitors. Another rally was scheduled the next day outside the home of **Raul Rivero**, director of Cuba Press. (RSF, CPJ, CubaNet, *El Nuevo Herald*)

The US administration granted licences to 10 US media organisations on 12 February to open news bureaux in Cuba. These include CNN, AP and the *Miami Herald*. This followed international pressure on the US government to respect the right of American media organisations to report on a permanent basis from Cuba. However, CNN is the only one of the 10 also to have permission from Cuba to open an office there. The Communist Party daily *Granma* rejected the US decision to grant the licences as a 'new act of interference by Washington'. (CPJ, IAPA, Reuters, AP)

## EGYPT

**Magdi Hussein**, editor-in-chief of *al-Sha'ab*, was imprisoned on 28 January after being found guilty and sentenced to one year's imprisonment for libelling the sons

of interior minister General Hassan al-Alfi. Hussein was given a year's suspended sentence in May 1996, which comes into effect following the latest conviction. (RSF)

Censors have lifted a ban on the staging of the play *A Visit to Heaven and Hell* by **Mustafa Mahmoud** although censorship board officials are attending rehearsals before making the final decision about whether the public can see it. The play depicts a murderous tyrant meeting three famous belly-dancers in heaven and the board has already ordered that Mahmoud remove the dancers' names from the text. Depiction of heaven and hell is a topic proscribed by Islam and the go-ahead is being seen as a possible precursor to bans being lifted on other works with religious themes. Mahmoud, however, claims that the censors' real objection to the play was its criticism of Marxist ideology. (Agence France-Presse)

The Constitutional Court on 2 February dismissed as unconstitutional an article in the penal code which imposes criminal responsibility for offences such as libel on editors-in-chief. However, they would be held responsible if they deliberately allowed publication of a libellous article, knowing its implications and consequences. (Egyptian Organization for Human Rights)

## ETHIOPIA

**Arega Wolde-Kirkos**, acting editor-in-chief of the inde-

pendent Amhari-language paper *Tobia*, was arrested without charge on 6 January. (IFJ)

Charges were filed on 15 January against 1,218 of the 1,800 detainees who have been in prison since the 1991 overthrow of the government of Mengistu Haile-Mariam. The charges arise in connection with the so-called Red Terror between 1977-78 in which thousands of people opposed to the Dergue military government were extrajudicially executed, disappeared or tortured. (AI, *Guardian*)

**Taye Belachew** (*Index* 1/1997), editor-in-chief of *Tobia*, deputy editor-in-chief **Anteneh Merid** and **Goshu Moges**, acting manager of the company which publishes the paper, were released from detention on 11 February. The terms of their release are not yet known. (CPJ)

## EUROPEAN UNION

On 19 February the European Court of Human Rights upheld Britain's prosecution of three men for causing injuries to each other during sadomasochistic sex, despite the fact that the men had consented to be injured. (*Times*)

## FRANCE

On 13 January *Paris-Match* was fined FF100,000 (US$18,000) under the privacy law for publishing photos of François Mitterrand's body only days after his death. (*Guardian*)

Several hundred artists, actors and film-makers demonstrated in Toulon during a court hearing on 13 February on the sacking of the left-wing theatre director **Gérard Paquet** and the attempted closure of his theatre and cultural centre at Chateauvallon by National Front mayor Jean-Marie Le Chevallier. Paquet, who had turned down a US$800,000 council subsidy and refused to accept the council's own programme, was accused of encouraging 'degenerate' projects such as black music and Jewish writing. Meanwhile, 155 writers and intellectuals have backed a protest by film-makers against new laws requiring citizens to report the arrival and departure of foreign guests without residence permits. (Reuters, *Guardian*, *Times*)

On 21 February a Paris court decided not to ban a poster advertising the film *The People vs Larry Flynt*, despite complaints that it was offensive to Christians. The film's director, Milos Forman, withdrew the posters voluntarily on 24 February. (Reuters)

### GERMANY

On 17 January prosecutors filed charges against Party of Democratic Socialism deputy leader, **Angela Marquardt**, on the grounds that she may have broken the law by linking her Internet homepage to the Netherlands-based Internet magazine *Radikal*, which contains material illegal in Germany. She could be charged with aiding and abet-

ting the original crime by allowing others access to *Radikal* (http://www.xs4all. nl/~radikal). (Reuters)

On 31 January city authorities in Frankfurt banned a demonstration against the Turkish government due to be held the following day, saying they believed the demonstration could by a vehicle for the outlawed **Kurdistan Workers' Party** (PKK). The authorities stated they had reason to believe PKK supporters from Belgium and the Netherlands had been mobilised to attend the protest, and that it constituted a 'grave threat to public safety'. Police prepared leaflets in German and Turkish telling demonstrators to turn back. (Reuters)

On 10 February **Hans-Christian Wendt**, editor of the neo-Nazi newspaper *Zeitung*, was convicted of disseminating unconstitutional propaganda and incitement to racial hatred and sentenced to one year's imprisonment. (Associated Press)

### GREECE

The trial of journalist **Dede Abduhalim** began on 20 February. He is charged with 'spreading false news which could cause distress and fear among citizens or weaken their faith in Greece'. The case arises from an article published in *Trakianin Sesi*, a newspaper serving the Muslim Turkish-speaking minority in Thrace. The article discussed a 'parallel state', a veiled reference to a mafia or police state, in the zone of

Komotini. Abduhalim has also been charged with setting up a radio station, Radio Isik, without official permission, although the majority of Greek stations broadcast without a licence. (RSF)

### HAITI

On 10 January a peaceful demonstration by 150 to 200 protesters demanding the resignation of the government was suppressed by the US-trained 'Force to Maintain Order' of the Haitian National Police. The police fired tear gas shells at the marchers, one of which exploded, blowing the hand off 23-year old Dieuseul Civil. The police defended the action, claiming that they had used 'appropriate force' against the marchers who were a 'little violent'. The police also claimed that the march was illegal. (Haitian Information Bureau)

### HONG KONG

Controversial artist **Pun Sing-lui** was banned from an Urban Council seminar at which he had been booked to speak in late January on the grounds that he had contravened the Council's principle of respecting works of art. Pun was gaoled in September for throwing a pot of red paint over a statue of Queen Victoria. (*South China Morning Post*)

On 1 February the Preparatory Committee for the Hong Kong Special Administrative Region provoked widespread condemnation when it approved plans

## DANANG KUKUH WARDOYO

# Lessons from prison

*On 16 March 1995 Danang Kukuh Wardoyo was arrested at the office of the Alliance of Independent Journalists (AJI), where he was working as an administrator (see* Index *5/1995). He had never been particularly interested in politics or journalism, but a year-and-a-half inside Indonesia's prison system changed that*

After finishing high school I left my home in Kediri, a small village in east Java, to fulfil my dream of going to university. Unfortunately I failed the exam, and, wanting to be independent, I went to find work in Jakarta while I waited to retake it. That's how I came to be in AJI's office, working as the office boy. At the same time I continued to study, still hoping to realise my ambition of further education.

But all my dreams were shattered when a group of plainclothes policemen dragged me away, without a warrant, for interrogation. Swearing and threatening, they accused me of helping AJI to sell their magazine, *Independen*, and said that I had been spreading hatred against the government. My case was submitted for trial and, during the pantomime that followed, I was sentenced to 20 months' imprisonment. I was 18 years old.

I spent my imprisonment in four different places: the police detention centre in central Jakarta, in Pondok Bambu, Salemba and, finally, Tangerang Prison for Young Offenders. The most terrifying of these was Pondok Bambu, where I was held in a quarantine cell four metres by four, along with 19 others. It really was hell in there.

I often dreamed of how great life must be for people outside those walls. Free to do whatever they wanted. While I, still so young, had to be locked up and cut off from the outside world for something I hadn't done. To reduce the boredom I began a new hobby — noting down interesting things that happened. There was always something to write about. I'm planning to use my notes to write a book.

In Tangerang Prison, towards the end of my imprisonment, I accidentally bumped into Meity Joseph, the prosecutor in my case. She came up to me and said: 'Will you forgive me? It really wasn't fair that you were tried. I was in the wrong.' I just shrugged my shoulders. There wasn't any need for words. The prosecutor, the judge, all of them are only civil servants who are subservient to their superiors. Which means that, in this country, what's true cannot always be spoken, and what's wrong can't always be acknowledged.

But the admission of that prosecutor made me believe in myself again. That I really wasn't in the wrong.

to repeal 16 laws and amend nine others, including the Bill of Rights. The proposed changes will resurrect many recently abolished restrictions. They include the restoration of police power to ban protests and the restriction of foreign funding for local activist groups. Hong Kong's governor-elect, Tung Chee-hwa, has declared his support for the plans and stressed the importance of social stability over individual rights. (AI, *Independent*, *International Herald Tribune*)

## HUNGARY

Prosecutors banned Hitler's *Mein Kampf* on 17 December 1996 in response to protests from Jewish groups at the advertising of a Hungarian translation in the far-right newspaper *Demokrata*. About 500 copies were sold before the banning, and the rest of the print run was subsequently confiscated. (*International Herald Tribune*)

## INDIA

The Supreme Court ruled on 12 December 1996 that the government must remove an estimated 44-100 million children, almost all Dalits, from working illegally in dangerous trades, in particular glass-making, firework manufacture and brass production. The ruling is based on an article of the Constitution which guarantees free education until the age of 14. The decision also affects millions of children working as bonded labourers. The court also ruled that children employed in non-hazardous jobs should

not work more than six hours a day and must receive at least two hours' schooling. (*Times*)

**Altaf Ahmed Faktoo**, a news broadcaster for Doordarshan, the government television station, was shot dead in Srinagar, Kashmir, on 1 January, probably by militant separatists. Seven journalists have been killed in Kashmir since 1990, of whom three worked for state-owned media. (CPJ)

## INDONESIA

**Muchtar Pakpahan**, leader of the unofficial Indonesian Prosperous Labour Union, **Budiman Sudjatmiko**, leader of the People's Democratic Party (PRD), and 11 other PRD activists went on trial on 12 December in four separate trials in Jakarta and Surabaya. Originally detained in connection with the 27 July Jakarta riots (*Index* 5/1996), all 13 have been charged under the anti-subversion law, accused of attempting to subvert President Suharto's regime and replace the state ideology. Muchtar has been charged in connection with his writings and statements, including his 1995 book *Potret Negara Indonesia* (Portrait of the Indonesian State) on trade union and social issues. (Tapol, ISAI, *Guardian*)

On 18 January five students were arrested in Purwokerto, Central Java, and accused of inciting crime. They had been distributing stickers calling for an election boycott unless wages were raised and

land evictions stopped. If found guilty they face up to five years in gaol. (HRW)

Authorities in West Java banned 135 minority religious groups in mid-January for causing unrest among mainstream religions. Sixty-one sects not deemed deviant have been allowed to continue. Meanwhile, police in the province announced that 42 people will stand trial for inciting the Tajikmalaya riots in December. The riots, which left four dead, began after reports of police brutality. (SWB, *Jakarta Post*, *Business Times*)

A book on the Jakarta riots of July 1996 was banned in early February by the military authorities in Central Java. Jointly published by the Alliance of Independent Journalists (AJI) and the Institute for the Studies on Free Flow of Information, *Peristiwa 27 Juli* (27 July Incident) details the violent takeover of PDI headquarters by the authorities and the resulting disturbances. Major-General Subagyo explained the ban on the grounds of the unofficial status of the publishers, saying 'if the institutions are banned so are their products'. (*Jakarta Post*)

New electioneering rules were announced on 4 February requiring campaigners' scripts to be checked by a government-sanctioned screening service before they can be broadcast. The screening, which will involve an estimated 900 scripts from the three competing parties, aims to ensure that candidates do not undermine state ideology, slander the government or other contenders during Indonesia's month-long campaigning season. (*Jakarta Post, International Herald Tribune*)

**Andi Syahputra** (*Index* 1/1997), business manager of the unlicensed paper *Suara Independen* (Voice of Independence), went on trial on 20 February charged with violating three articles of the criminal code covering the crimes of 'hate-sowing' and insulting the president or vice-president. Sentences range from 16 months to six years. (CCPJ, HRW, ISAI)

Ousted PDI leader **Megawati Soekarnoputri** was questioned on 20 February over a political meeting held at her house on 10 January to celebrate the 24th anniversary of the founding of her party. The meeting took place without police permission, after Megawati's request for a permit was reportedly returned unanswered. Megawati and her supporters have been excluded from the government-approved list of PDI candidates in the forthcoming election. (Reuters)

## IRAN

**Faraj Sarkoohi** (*Index* 6/1996, 1/1997), editor-in-chief of the monthly literary magazine *Adineh*, was formally arrested on 27 January by information service agents in Tehran. He is being held incommunicado. After disappearing on 3 November shortly before boarding a plane to Germany, he reappeared in Tehran in late

December. A letter written by Sarkoohi on 3 January, and smuggled out of Iran after his arrest, details his captivity. Sarkoohi says that his captors forced him to incriminate himself as a spy with connections to the French and German cultural attachés in Tehran in a series of videotaped interviews. In a telephone call to Sarkoohi's wife in mid-February, his brother Esma'il, who is also being detained in Iran, urged her to reject the document as a forgery. (Iranian PEN Centre in Exile, A19, AI)

On 12 February security surrounding British novelist **Salman Rushdie** was stepped up when the 15th Khordad (June Fifth) Foundation increased the bounty for his murder to US$2.5 million. The newspaper *Jomhuri Islami* ran a 15-page supplement on Rushdie on the anniversary of the *fatwa*, including a caricature of him digging his own grave with a pen. (*Guardian*)

## IRELAND

On 13 January the Circuit Civil Court decided it was not necessary to imprison *Daily Star* journalist **Barry O'Kelly** for refusing to reveal his sources. O'Kelly had declined to identify his source for an article which led to a claim for breach of contract being brought against the Garda Representative Association by a former employee. The court found that it was able to settle the case without identifying the source of O'Kelly's information. (*Irish Times*)

## JORDAN

**Omar Nadi**, editor of the satirical weekly *Abed Rabbo*, was arrested on 24 January after a member of Parliament, Ibrahim Kilani, and the minister of public works, Abdul Hadi Majali, both filed libel charges against him. Kilani complained about a cartoon that depicted him wishing to join the government while the minister objected to the title 'General' that the magazine had given him (a reference to his former role as head of the security services) and the implication that he is a thief. (RSF)

Two journalists were given prison sentences in January. **Na'el Salah**, editor of weekly *al-Haqiqah*, was sentenced to nine months for 'distributing false information', 'infringing morality and ethics' and 'publishing pornographic material' because of reports about an Amman amusement park. **Abdullah Bani Issa**, editor of weekly *al-Hayat*, was sentenced to six months for 'insulting the King and his family' because of an interview with an Islamist leader published in weekly *al-Hiwar* in October 1995. He is free on bail pending appeal. (RSF)

## KAZAKHSTAN

The body of **Chris Gehring**, director of the Internews Network Agency, was found in his apartment on 9 January. Police believe he was killed by burglars, although his colleagues say there may be a political motive for the murder. Three suspects were apprehended

• • • • • • • • • • • • • • • • • • • • • • • • • • • • • • • •

## FARAJ SARKOOHI

# For my wife and children

'Today is 14th *Dey* 1375 [3 January 1997]. I, Faraj Sarkoohi, am writing down this account in great haste in the hope that people one day will be able to read it, and that the world, the Iranian public and not least my wife Farideh and my children, Arash and Bahar, whom I love most intensely, will discover what a terrifying ordeal I have been dragged into.

'I don't know how much time I have. I expect to be re-arrested at any moment or to be murdered in such a way that it will be made to look like suicide. Prison, torture and death are what lie ahead of me. In writing down these notes, I have to concentrate on what has actually happened, although I yearn to describe exactly what goes on inside me and how I feel. But for whoever reads this account it will be possible to some extent to imagine my predicament...

'When they took me to prison on the 13th of *Aban* [3 November 1996], interrogation and torture started right away. From the very first day they told me: "You have been reported missing. It has been made officially known that you have left the country and your arrival has been registered at the airport in Hamburg. You will be kept here in isolation and when the interrogations, the interviews and our inquiries are over we are going to kill you and bury your body in secret or let it be found somewhere in Germany."

'On the third or fourth day they played me a recorded telephone conversation in which my brother, Esma'il, told my wife, Farideh, that the airport's information bureau had confirmed my departure from Iran. They played me the tape to convince me that they are not lying. Under severe

on 15 January. On 3 February, Internews announced the creation of the Chris Gehring Memorial Fund to aid journalists in central Asia. The fund will also be used to continue Gehring's work and will include an annual prize for journalists and a legal defence fund for journalists working in the area. (CPJ, SWB)

On 24 January the upper house of Parliament discussed a draft of the new language law already passed by the lower house, which aims to increase the use of Kazakh. Even though Kazakh is officially the state language, legislators say its status is still lower than Russian. The bill gives ethnic Kazakhs in the government until 2005 to master the language and 2010 for ethnic Russians. (OMRI, SWB)

**Charles Kuria Wamwere**, brother of Koigi wa Wamwere (*Index* 2/1995, 2/1996, 5/1996, 1/1997), and former army captain **Geoffrey Njuguna Ngengi** were granted bail on medical grounds on 13 January. They are receiving treatment in hospital and awaiting their appeal against a four-year gaol term. (NDIMA, AI) pressure and torture I was interrogated and forced to give interviews. They provided the texts and I had to repeat them...

'They said they would release me for a certain period on condition that I did everything that they wanted. I agreed. Anything, even death or my rearrest — which will surely come perhaps even today or tomorrow — seemed preferable to the situation I was in. They told me they planned to let me appear at Mehrabad airport and be interviewed by journalists. On this occasion I did not believe anything they said. They obtained documents about my supposed trip to Turkmenistan. They told me what to say and how to answer journalists' questions.

'At Mehrabad airport, I gave interviews that were published and made public. I said what they [the Ministry of Intelligence] ordered. Subsequently I had interviews with the BBC and French radio telling them — and for that matter everyone else — what I had been ordered to say, the same things I said at the airport. I have not let anyone, not even my brother, know the truth. There is nothing I can do.

'I don't know if anyone will ever set eyes on this note. I am certain that sooner or later they will come for me and I will be imprisoned and most probably killed. But I have no clues as to what I can do about it. I am not even sure what to do with this long note. Maybe I will tear it up in the end. I believe it would never reach anyone. But deep down I have a burning wish that Farideh and my children will come to read it. That they shall find out how I have suffered and would not believe for a moment that I have been a spy...'

*Translated by Ahmad Ebrahimi, Iranian PEN Centre in Exile*

*The full version of this letter appears on our website (http://www.oneworld.org/index_oc/news/)*

● ● ● ● ● ● ● ● ● ● ● ● ● ● ● ● ● ● ● ● ● ● ● ● ● ● ● ● ● ● ● ●

**Rebecca Nduku**, a photographer for the *Nation* newspaper, was hospitalised on 19 January after being attacked by a senior police officer while she was covering an interdenominational service in a Nairobi slum village. The *Nation's* newsroom driver, **Alphonse Muthoka**, was also beaten by police officers as he attempted to call for help on the car radio. (NDIMA)

Joshua Kulei, a businessman and member of President Moi's Cabinet, filed a defamation lawsuit against the *People* on 31 January for an article published in the 24-30 January edition which associated him with a group of Asian businessmen who allegedly solicit government favours. State House deputy comptroller John Lolorio is also suing the paper over the same article. (NDIMA)

Recent publications: *Justice on Trial — the Koigi Case* (Koigi wa Wamwere, Views Media, 1996); *Detention, Torture and Health Professionals* (AI, January 1997, 24pp)

**KUWAIT**

On 29 December 1996 five Islamist deputies introduced a bill seeking to ban concerts and fashion shows in Kuwait. Violations of the ban would be punishable by a prison term of up to six months, a fine of at least 5,000 dinars (US$16,000) and the closure of the facility used to hold the event. Islamists have attacked the government for allowing concerts after a five-year ban following the 1990-91 Iraqi occupation of Kuwait. Kuwait already bans public dancing and alcohol. (*Guardian*)

## KYRGYZSTAN

The Justice Ministry ordered the Uchkun printing house to cease producing the new independent paper *Kriminal* on 17 January, one week after the paper's first issue appeared. The Ministry cited problems over the paper's licence registration. Prime Minister Jumaguov announced his intention to sue *Kriminal* over an article in the first issue which accused him of building a private home on the site of an old cemetery outside the capital. Pervomaysky District Court in Bishkek ordered the paper to close on 10 February, pending the outcome of the case. (CPJ)

The Movement for Deliverance from Poverty in Kyrgyzstan applied on 21 January to become an official opposition party. The Movement held its founding congress in December 1996, after which one of its leaders, **Jumagazy Usupov**, was gaoled for 15 days. Another founder of the movement, **Topchubek Turgunaliyev**, was given a 10-year prison sentence on charges of fraud. He was accused of embez-

zling US$10,000 from Bishkek University for the Humanities. The university, however, says that this was a loan which Turgunaliyev had promised to return with interest. Opposition leaders believe the case against him is politically motivated. *Res Publica* correspondent **Ryspek Omurzakov** (*Index* 5/1996) recieved an official warning on 14 February in connection with his coverage of Turgunaliyev's trial. (OMRI, HRW)

## MALAYSIA

Penang authorities have adopted stiff new sentencing for criminal offences under *sharia* law. Punishments announced in December 1996 include caning for prostitution, incest, adultery and homosexuality, and increased fines and gaol terms for *khalwat*, or close proximity (*Index* 1/1997). (*Straits Times*)

On 14 January officers of the Malaysian Registrar of Companies raided the offices of human rights group **Tenaganita**, the **Institute of Social Analysis**, and the **Selangor Chinese Assembly Hall**, seizing documents and questioning staff members. The raids, described as 'routine inspections' by the officers, are believed to be part of a government initiative to crack down on NGOs. (Reuters, *Straits Times*)

In early February prime minister Mahathir Mohamad announced a crackdown on teenagers found smoking or in possession of cigarettes and

tobacco, with effect from early March, as part of a crusade against moral decay and western influence. Those caught face fines ranging from US$18 to US$380. (*Guardian*)

## MALDIVES

**Mohamed Shaheeb**, a journalist with the paper *Haveeru*, was arrested on 20 January, apparently in connection with a fictional story he wrote, entitled 'Kuda Golhi' (The Interrogation Room). The story depicts the treatment of a young woman held in solitary confinement in a police cell. (AI)

## MAURITANIA

Independent weekly *al-Akhbar* was seized at the printing press in January by government officials from the Political Affairs and Public Freedoms Office acting under Article 11 of the press law. No reason was given. On 15 December the paper was banned because of a report on AIDS prevention among prostitutes in Nouakchott. Since December 1996 *La Tribune*, *L'Eveil-Hebdo*, and *El Messah* have all been seized without explanation. An edition of *Mauritanie-Nouvelles* (*Index* 5/1996), which carried an article linking an official with drug trafficking and racist comments by a minister, was seized on 30 December. (RSF)

## MEXICO

**Fernando Balderas**, a journalist with *Cuarto Poder*, his wife **Yolanda Figueroa**, a journalist and writer, and their three sons were found murdered in their home in El Pedregal de San Angel on 5 December 1996. The federal district prosecutor believes the motive for the murders was revenge. Figueroa had caused a scandal in Mexico when she wrote a book accusing the government of postponing the capture of the ringleader of the Cartel del Golfo, Juan García Abrego, who was later extradited to the USA. (IFJ, Reuters)

**Yuri González Pérez**, photographer with the Ciudad Juarez daily *El Norte*, disappeared on 8 January while on his way to report on snowstorms in northern Mexico. He has not been seen since. In 1996 three photographers with *El Norte* were assaulted in the same area where González is thought to have disappeared. (IAPA)

On 27 January **Mary Pérez de Soto**, church secretary to **Fr Camilo Daniel**, and her two children fled into hiding following a series of anonymous threats to kill both her son and Fr Daniel if the priest continued his work as president of the Commission for Solidarity and the Defence of Human Rights. No action has been taken by the authorities to investigate the death threats. It is feared that this campaign of intimidation is part of a wider pattern of such campaigns against social and human rights activists in Mexico. (AI)

## MOROCCO

The Arabic weekly *al-*
*Mustakillah* was seized on 25 January and banned from distribution. No official reason was given but Fathi Belhaj, the newspaper's correspondent in Rabat, said: 'We believe a six-page report on Muslim fundamentalists' activity in Morocco contained in the issue was the target of the seizure.' The paper is printed in London and distributes several hundred copies in Morocco. (Reuters)

Over 100 students from Muhammad V University in Casablanca were arrested in January following demonstrations against poor housing and transport facilities. Among those arrested were three leaders of the National Union of Moroccan Students who were sentenced on 24 January to between one and three years' imprisonment on charges of threatening public order, attacking policemen and damaging public property. The university, which has 30,000 students, is known for its support for the banned Islamic party, **al-Adl wa al-Ihssane** (Justice and Spirituality). By early February at least 46 students had been sentenced to prison terms from between three months to two years. Many were students at other universities who had demonstrated in solidarity with the Casablanca students. (Moroccan Press Agency, *Times*)

## NAMIBIA

On 29 January Alpheus Naruseb, Swapo's secretary for information and publicity,
called homosexuality 'a hideous deviation' to be 'uprooted totally as a practice' from Namibian society. This followed similar remarks made by President Nujoma at a Swapo Women's Congress on 6 December. A group including the women's group Sister Namibia and the Gay and Lesbian Organisation of Namibia (GLON) condemned Naruseb's remarks as hate speech. (MISA, *Namibian*)

## NEW ZEALAND

The Internet Society of New Zealand (ISONZ) and the Internal Affairs Department (IA) set up a joint working group to tackle pornography on the Internet in December 1996. This followed several high-profile raids and monitoring exercises by the authorities. The ISONZ is also developing a code of practice for Internet service providers. (*Independent*)

In January the Film and Literature Board of Review overturned a decision made by the Office of Film and Literature Classification in August 1996 to ban a giant cut-out of the naked Vegas Girl. The billboard has been a landmark of Auckland's redlight district for the past 20 years. (Reuters)

## NIGERIA

**Godwin Agbroko**, editor-in-chief of the independent paper the *Week*, was detained on 18 December 1996 and is being held incommunicado in Abuja following an article in the 16-23 December edition about a dispute between senior military officers. (AI, PEN, RSF)

On 24 January information minister Walter Ofonagoro announced government plans to set up a press court to try journalists who 'report untruths' and to enforce Decree 43, issued in 1993, which requires newspapers to renew their publishing licences every year. (CPJ, Inter Press Service, Reuters)

**Ernest Udokang**, an editor with the state-controlled Radio Service of Akwa Ibom, was suspended for one month without pay on 1 February following a commentary on the national immigration programme, which was broadcast on 27 January. The commentary was ordered to be discontinued after its first broadcast because of complaints of 'distaste' by Iyabo Adeusi, the wife of the state's military administrator. (Independent Journalism Centre)

The Federal Secretariat in Abuja — a complex housing most of the federal ministries — is reported to have issued a ban on women who visit or work there from wearing trousers. (*West Africa*)

### NORTH KOREA

A ban on foreign travel for officials was announced on 15 February, three days after the shock defection of senior government adviser Hwang Jang Yop as he returned from a trip to Japan. Officials travelling to Beijing were reportedly ordered off their train

just before the Chinese border, while a Foreign Ministry delegation also has found its travel plans cancelled. (*Independent*)

Recent publication: *Public Executions — Converging Testimonies* (AI, January 1997, 15pp)

### PAKISTAN

A bomb blast on 18 January outside the Sessions Court in Lahore killed **ZA Shahid**, a press photographer for *Khabrain*, and injured five other journalists. The bomb was meant for the leaders of Sipah Sahaba Pakistan, an anti-Shi'ite religious-political party. (Pakistan Press Foundation)

**Zahid Ali Qaimkhani**, a journalist with the news agency Pakistan Press International, was released from prison on 21 January after the Sindh High Court granted his appeal against a conviction for setting fire to the local telephone exchange. Qaimkhani believes he was framed in retaliation for his articles on corruption among the local government administration. (Pakistan Press Foundation)

Nearly 200 Christians were detained by police in Karachi on 13 February during a protest against attacks on churches in Punjab earlier in the month. Police broke up the demonstration with tear gas and batons. (*Times*)

An armed mob ransacked the offices of the Urdu daily *Assas* in Rawalpindi on 16

February because the paper had refused to publish the statement of a candidate standing in the provincial assembly elections earlier in the month. The mob damaged furniture and equipment and stole US$5,000. (Pakistan Press Foundation)

### PALESTINE (AUTONOMOUS AREAS)

Palestinian students from Gaza are still unable to attend West Bank universities because of travel restrictions which prevent them travelling through Israel. Around 1,200 students have been prevented from reaching their universities since the closures imposed in March 1996. (B'Tselem)

Recent publication: *The Clashes of September 1996 — Investigation into the Causes and the Use of Force* (Palestinian Centre for Human Rights, January 1997, 130pp)

### PAPUA NEW GUINEA

Following an angry public reaction to the controversial National Information and Communication Bill and Media Commission Bill, the Constitutional Review Commission has decided to allow the media to regulate themselves rather than impose statutory licensing, registration and regulatory bodies. The bills will now be redrafted accordingly. (Pacific Islands News Association)

The National Court in Mount Hagen ruled in mid-February that the payment of 'living men or women' in compensation cases is unlawful. **Miriam Willingal**, 18, bought the action when her relatives decided she would be given away in marriage, with 24 pigs and US$20 in cash, as part of a traditional death compensation payment to a neighbouring tribe. The courts ruled that such action was an infringement of her rights to equal treatment and freedom to marry according to choice. (*Sydney Morning Herald*)

## PERU

**Hitomi Tsuyoshi**, correspondent for the Japanese station TV Asahi, and his translator **Victor Borja** were detained by police on 7 January. Their equipment was also confiscated. They were released four days later having been held without charge by the National Anti-Terrorism Agency. Their confiscated equipment was handed over to the Japanese embassy. The pair had been detained after gaining unauthorised entrance to the Japanese ambassador's Lima residence where the Tupac Amaru Revolutionary Movement are holding 74 people hostage. (AMARC, Instituto Prensa y Sociedad)

On 7 January **Miguel Bravo Quispe**, was found shot dead in the barrio of Buenos Aires. Bravo was vice-president of the Pasco College of Journalists and a correspondent with the daily *El Comercio*. He was also mayor of the district of Yanancancha, close to Cerro de Pasco. (Instituto Prensa y Sociedad)

## PHILIPPINES

**Roberto Berbon**, a senior editor at DZMM radio station, was shot dead by three unidentified gunmen on 15 December 1996. His wife was also wounded in the attack, which took place outside their home in Cavite Province. Berbon, the leader of a local anti-crime organisation, was the third journalist to be killed in 1996 and the sixth since President Ramos took office in 1992. (*International Herald Tribune*, CPJ, RSF)

In mid-January a critically acclaimed Filipino film about prostitution, *Call Me Happiness*, was given an 'X' rating, effectively preventing it being shown in public. Sex scenes and risqué subject matter prompted the Manila censors' decision, which has been widely criticised by members of the film industry. (*South China Morning Post, Straits Times*)

## POLAND

On 2 January it was reported that **Aleksander Checko**, editor-in-chief of Warsaw's daily *Zycie Warszawy*, and his deputy, **Karol Malcuzynski**, have been charged with disclosing state secrets and hampering proceedings in the Oleksy case last year. In spring 1996 the newspaper published a list of official and confidential reasons for dropping espionage proceedings against the former prime minister, and revealed the identity of Grigoriy Yakimishin, a Russian agent working with the Polish authorities. The journalists refused to disclose their information sources. (SWB)

It was reported on 10 January that journalists in the state and private media are to be screened for co-operation with the Communist-era secret service, according to a decision by the Sejm commission responsible for drafting the lustration law. (OMRI)

## RUSSIAN FEDERATION

*Russia:* It was announced in early December 1996 that the Academy of Sciences and the Centre for Gender Issues are seeking damages for the publication in Moscow's *Playboy* of provocative portraits of eminent women from Russian history, such as Catherine the Great, Natalya Goncharova, seventeenth-century religious dissident Feodosiva Morozova and the nineteenth-entury mathematician Sofia Korvalevskaya. (*Times*)

On 14 December 1996 **Aleksandr Nikitin**, the Russian co-author of the Bellona environmental report warning of the threat of radiation posed by the Russian northern fleet (*Index* 3/1996, 5/1996, 1/1997) was released from prison pending further investigation of his case. He remains charged with high treason through espionage and is not allowed to travel outside St Petersburg while awaiting trial. (*Ekspress Khronika*, PEN, AAASHRAN, OMRI)

Hearings began on 28 January

in the case against **Ilya Lazarenko**, charged with 'committing intentional actions aimed at national and racial emnity, humiliating national honour and dignity, propaganda of the exclusiveness of citizens on the basis of national or racial affiliation'. Lazarenko is the editor of the unregistered newspaper *Narodny Stroy* (Popular Order), a publication of the National Front. The prosecution is accusing Lazarenko of promoting racial and nationalist tension. (*Ekspress Khronika*)

**Vyacheslav Zvonarev**, editor of the Kursk independent television company Takt, was attacked late on 11 February and died later in hospital. His colleagues believe the attack was connected with his work. And **Vadim Biryukov**, founder of the business journal *Delvoye Lyudi*, was found dead in his garage on 25 February. He had been bound with tape and badly beaten. Police say that robbery is the probable motive for his murder. (OMRI, SWB)

*Chechnya:* On 18 January leaders of the right-wing party Ukrainian National Assembly (UNA) claimed they had discovered the whereabouts of **Vitaly Shevchenko**, a Kharkov television journalist who disappeared in Chechnya in August 1996 (*Index* 6/1996). He is reported to be in the Investigative Isolation Prison (SIZO) of the Russian Federal Security Service (FSB) in Vladikavkaz. The charges against him are

unknown. Journalists **Elena Petrova** and **Yuri Bazarluk** who disappeared with Shevchenko have not been found. (*Ekspress Khronika*, SWB)

Two Russian journalists from Russian Public Television (ORT), correspondent **Roman Perevezentsev** and cameraman **Vyacheslav Tibelius**, were taken hostage near Grozny on 19 January while on assignment covering the Chechen presidential election campaign. They were subsequently released on 17 February. (CPJ, RSF, SWB)

## RWANDA

Froduald Karamira, former vice-president of the Hutu party MDR-Power and a leader of the *interahamwe* militia, has been found guilty of inciting genocide through hate speech in repeated broadcasts on the extremist Hutu station **Radio Libre des Mille Collines** (RTLM). He was sentenced to death on 14 February. (*Guardian*, Reuters)

The Interior Ministry ordered the expulsion on 9 February of **Christian Jennings**, a Reuters correspondent based in Rwanda, following a Reuters report about a news conference on 7 February given by the deputy president, Paul Kagame. (Reuters)

Recent publication: *Human Rights Overlooked in Mass Repatriation* (AI, January 1997, 17pp); *Witness to Genocide — Joseph Ruyenzi: Prisoner Without a Conscience*

(African Rights, January 1997, 46pp)

## SAUDI ARABIA

On 6 February the Interior Ministry warned pilgrims that they would face tough punishment if they carried political material at the annual Muslim pilgrimage due in April. The Ministry asked pilgrims not to carry any books, pictures or publications that have 'a political or propaganda aim'. 'Anybody found to be in possession of anything forbidden', it continued, 'will be severely punished... without any leniency or toleration.' The Ministry issues similar warnings every year. (Reuters)

## SERBIA-MONTENEGRO

At least eight journalists and media workers were assaulted by police during an opposition demonstration in Belgrade on 2 February. **Sergei Karazei**, a Ukrainian cameraman for Reuters TV, was beaten by anti-riot police officers and had his camera damaged. **Predrag Vujic**, a journalist with Beta News Agency, and **Marko Petrovich** from *Blic* were beaten despite having shown police their press identification cards. **Maja Vidakovic**, cameraman **Savo Ilic** and assistant **Vvanja Lazin** from the private Belgrade television station BK were also assaulted. **Rainer Herscher**, a German cameraman for APTV, was also assaulted; and **Maria Fleet**, a camerawoman for the Belgrade office of CNN, had her camera damaged. (RSF, CPJ)

# Subscribe!

## United Kingdom & Overseas (excluding USA & Canada)

| | | UK: | | Overseas: | |
|---|---|---|---|---|---|
| **1 year** (6 issues) | | | £38 | | £43 |
| **2 years** (12 issues) | | | £66 | | £79 |
| **3 years** (18 issues) | | | £96 | | £114 |

Name

Address

B7A2

£ _____ total.  ❑ Cheque (£)  ❑ Visa/MC  ❑ Am Ex  ❑ Bill me

Card No.

Expiry        Signature

❑ I would also like to send **INDEX** to a reader in the developing
  world—just £25.

❑ I do not wish to receive mail from other companies.

**INDEX**, 33 Islington High St, London N1 9LH

# Subscribe!

## United States and Canada

| | US: | |
|---|---|---|
| **1 year** (6 issues) | | $50 |
| **2 years** (12 issues) | | $93 |
| **3 years** (18 issues) | | $131 |

Name

Address

B7B2

$ _____ total.  ❑ Cheque ($)  ❑ Visa/MC  ❑ Am Ex  ❑ Bill me

Card No.

Expiry        Signature

❑ I would also like to send **INDEX** to a reader in the developing
  world—just $35.

❑ I do not wish to receive mail from other companies.

 **INDEX**  33 Islington High St, London N1 9LH
Tel: 0171 278 2313 Fax: 0171 278 1878
Email: indexoncenso@gn.apc.org

## INDEX ON CENSORSHIP
33 Islington High Street
London N1 9BR
United Kingdom

## BUSINESS REPLY MAIL
FIRST CLASS  PERMIT NO.7796  NEW YORK, NY

Postage will be paid by addressee.

## INDEX ON CENSORSHIP
708 Third Avenue
8th Floor
New York, NY 10164-3005

## SIERRA LEONE

*Expo Times* editor-in-chief **Ibrahim Seaga Shaw** and acting editor **Charles Roberts** were released without charge on 23 December. They had been detained on 18 December following an article in that day's issue reporting an announcement by government radio of an alleged coup attempt. (CPJ)

**Pat Kawa**, a correspondent with *Punch* based in the second city Bo, was arrested and charged with four counts of defamation on 24 January, following an article about corruption among government officials in the region. He was released on bail. (CPJ)

## SINGAPORE

Opposition candidates and potential opposition voters came under attack in the run-up to the parliamentary elections on 2 January. Shortly before the start of campaigning the prime minister Goh Chok Tong warned that constituencies which voted for the opposition would not benefit from state spending on upgrading public housing. Meanwhile **Tang Liang Hong**, Workers' Party candidate in Cheng San, found himself demonised as a 'racist' and a danger to the delicate balance of the island's Malay, Chinese and Indian communities. His car was followed and his life threatened. Thirteen defamation suits were subsequently brought by 11 present or former ministers against Tang for anti-government remarks made

during his campaign. In preparation for the cases, a court injunction was issued in late January freezing Tang's assets, he and his wife were ordered to set aside US$7.9 million to cover damages and an official receiver was appointed to investigate the family on 17 February. Eight suits have also been filed against the leader of his party, **JB Jeyaretnam**. Defamation suits and financial investigations are a traditional government response to opposition figures: Jeyaretnam was bankrupted by actions brought against him after he won a seat in the previous elections. The People's Action Party, which has won all eight elections held since independence in 1965, has never lost a defamation case. (*Times, Guardian*, Reuters)

## SOUTH KOREA

Unions reacted angrily to labour legislation rushed through Parliament at a secret session held at 6am on 26 December 1996. Twenty amendments to labour law, restricting trade union organisations and removing existing job security, were passed by the ruling New Korea Party in the absence of the opposition. Riot police were deployed to break up the ensuing protests, five union leaders were detained between 11 and 23 January and warrants issued (but later suspended) for the arrest of 15 others. A delegation from the International Confederation of Free Trade Unions, who travelled to Seoul in support of the strikers, were threatened with expulsion on

15 January if they continued to address rallies and engage in 'activities disturbing public peace and order'. Although the strikes have come to an apparent end, unions continue to demand the repeal of the new laws, which make it easier to sack workers and replace strikers. (IFJ, AI, *Far Eastern Economic Review*)

## SRI LANKA

Two executives of Telshan Network Ltd (TNL), **Shan Wickramasinghe**, the director and **Ishini Wickramasinghe Perera**, the news director, were questioned by police officers on 31 December after the station broadcast a report concerning an operation by the Tamil Tigers. The same news item was broadcast by state radio and television, but the police took no action against them. Perera was arrested and interrogated under the Prevention of Terrorism Act (PTA). It is reported that on 17 January President Kumaratunga expressed her opposition to the use of the PTA against journalists. (Reuters, Free Media Movement)

**Fr Tissa Balasuriya**, a Colombo-based Catholic priest and theologian, was excommunicated by the Vatican at the beginning of January. He was accused of deviation from the faith for publishing a pamphlet questioning the Church's teaching on original sin and salvation. Fr Balasuriya's tract *Mary and Human Liberation* was published in 1990. (*Guardian*)

**Srinath Perare**, editor of the

paper *Aramuna*, was beaten by activists from the People's Liberation Front (JVP) on 22 January. Perare was covering a public meeting organised by the JVP in Colombo.

### SUDAN

**Nur al-Din Medani**, office manager of the paper *al-Khaleej*, is among about 50 people who have been arbitrarily detained without charge or trial in Khartoum since 13 January. (AI, OMCT)

On 14 January **Gaspar Biro**, the UN special rapporteur on Sudan, was expelled from the country by the government on the grounds that his safety could not be guaranteed. (AI)

Recent publication: *Beset by Contradictions — Islamisation, Legal Reform and Human Rights in Sudan* (Lawyers' Committee for Human Rights, 98pp)

### SWAZILAND

**Richard Nxumalo, Jan Sithole, Jabulani Nxumalo** and **Themba Msibi**, senior leaders of the Swaziland Federation of Trade Unions (SFTU), were charged on 3 February with the non-bailable offence of disrupting public order by intimidating bus drivers into participating in a national strike. The men were arrested on 31 January, three days before the beginning of the strike, which the SFTU called to force King Mswati III to agree to democratic reforms. The bus drivers union has denied that its members were forced to take part in the strike. (OMCT, SWB, AI)

On the weekend of 1 February unidentified people circulated pamphlets in Mbabane and Manzini which contained threats to journalists who reported favourably on the government during the national strike. The opposition People's United Democratic Movement (PUDEMO) denied reports in the state-funded *Swaziland Observer* that it was the source of the pamphlets. On 7 February the Mbabane offices of **Tom Holloway**, a correspondent for the South African Press Agency and the BBC, were broken into and US$3,000 worth of equipment was stolen. (MISA, South African Press Agency)

A blanket ban on coverage and any statements and announcements of the strike by state-controlled radio and television broadcasters was allegedly ordered by the cabinet on 3 February. The ban was reportedly implemented under the terms of the Criminal Procedure and Evidence Act, drafted and passed on 2 February, which bans all material likely to 'incite the public against the government'. (MISA)

### SWITZERLAND

On 29 December 1996 legal authorities admitted to having tapped the telephone and fax lines of the Sunday magazine *Sonntagsblick* between 1 and 25 September, in order to identify the source of the leaks which led to the magazine's publication of a confi-dential report dealing with the financing of state welfare programmes. The telephone of the report's author was also tapped. (RSF)

### TIBET

On 20 December 1996 the Tibet State Security Office banned a number of Hollywood film stars thought to support Tibetan independence. Those blacklisted include Harrison Ford, Martin Scorsese, Brad Pitt, and French director Jean-Jacques Annaud, all of whom have been recently involved in films on Tibet. (*Times*)

On 26 December Tibetan exile **Ngawang Choepel** was sentenced to 18 years' imprisonment on charges of spying for the Dalai Lama's government-in-exile and the USA. Ngawang's sentence is one of the longest to be handed down for a political crime in recent years. (Tibet Information Network, *International Herald Tribune*)

### TOGO

**Abass Dermane**, editor-in-chief of the weekly *Le Regard*, was detained at the Ministry of the Interior on 4 February and held for four days. He was accused of 'disturbing public order' and 'defaming the head of state' following an article alleging human rights violations under the regime of President Eyadema published in the 14 January edition. The 5 February edition of the paper was seized. (RSF, CPJ)

**Augustin Assiobo**, editor-in-

# OCAK ISIK YURTÇU

# The spirit of journalism

*A former editor of the banned paper* Özgür Gündem, *Ocak Isik Yurtçu is currently serving 15 years in prison for charges under the anti-terror law. In December last year both Reporters Sans Frontières and the Committee to Protect Journalists gave Yurtçu awards in recognition of his work. CPJ commended his 'extraordinary devotion to the principles of press freedom through extensive and balanced reporting of the Kurdish conflict'*

'I have some health problems. I suffer from rheumatism and I should be under continuous medical care. But I'm being pressured by the authorities to apply for a presidential pardon on health grounds. They would prefer I was free, instead of being a prisoner of conscience with international support. And since they can't change the laws under which I was jailed, they are looking for other ways to get me out.

'I've been locked up with 23 young political prisoners. They are very respectful and try to make things easier for me. I'm rather a strange prisonmate for the common prisoners, though. One day they see a cartoon strip about me printed in a daily paper; then I'm visited by hordes of journalists; then someone comes and gives me a Freedom of the Press award. And they ask: "Who is this man who has suddenly become so important? We hardly receive a letter a year, while he's getting awards every day!"

'Last week I got a letter from Mexico City, from my first girlfriend, who I knew more than 30 years ago. She had come across a story about me in a Turkish paper which she had managed to find there. You can imagine how nice that was.

'During the day the other political prisoners generally sleep so that they can read when the dormitory is at its quietest, but my routine is the opposite. I'm a 52-year-old man, I have habits. I get up at six o'clock, have my daily exercise, have a cup of tea. Then the newspapers come, and I start the "proof-reading" — as if I'm the editor-in-chief, I start correcting them all with a red pen. An hour later, the batch of papers looks like a bunch of red tulips.

'By the time I was put in prison I'd actually retired and was planning just to write the occasional article. But now the spirit of journalism has been reawakened. It's 30 years since I began my career, but I'm keener than ever not just to practise journalism, but also to carry on the fight for press freedom.'

*Interviewed by Nadire Mater*

chief of the weekly *Tingo-Tingo* was detained on 5 February and accused of 'defamation' and 'making death threats' following a complaint lodged by the family of the former external affairs minister, Alasounouma Boumbera. (RSF)

## TUNISIA

Lawyer and human rights activist **Najib Hosni** (*Index* 1/1997) and **Mohamed Hedi Sassi**, a member of the the Tunisian Workers' Communist Party, were released conditionally on 14 December after more than two years in prison. **Mohamed Mouadda** and **Khemais Chammari** (*Index* 5/1996) were also given conditional releases on 30 December. (AI)

## TURKEY

On 23 January officers from the Anti-Terror Branch of Istanbul police raided the Kurdish-owned Komal Publishing House in Istanbul. They confiscated large amounts of equipment including floppy disks and computers, and detained publishers **Kadir Satik** and **Mete Demirkol**. Satik was subsequently released. Demirkol was formally arrested and committed to prison to await trial. (AI)

The Turkish authorities have stepped up harassment of viewers of **Med-TV**, the Kurdish-language satellite TV station. Following a meeting of Turkey's National Security Council the Ankara Security Directorate on 30 January

demanded the names of buyers of satellite dishes from electronic equipment shops. On 12 February Necati Bilican, governor of Turkey's state of emergency area, threatened the banning of satellite dishes in Kurdish-speaking regions. In some areas police have removed dishes; in others, Med-TV viewers report having had their houses marked by the police. (Med-TV)

On 5 February **Bekir Yildiz**, Islamist mayor of Ankara's Sincan district, was taken by police for questioning. Yildiz enraged secularists in Turkey after hosting a day of anti-Israel protests in Sincan which culminated in calls for the implementation of *sharia* law. (Reuters)

The centre-left daily *Radikal* was seized on 17 February in connection with an article, reprinted from the French weekly *Figaro Magazine*, entitled 'Turkey: Army against the Islamists' and written by Islamist intellectual Abdurrahman Dilipak. The article described the founder of modern Turkey, Kemal Ataturk, as 'an authoritarian military ruler'. (RSF)

## TURKMENISTAN

**Marat Durdyev**, a prominent journalist and author, was forcibly incarcerated in a psychiatric hospital in Ashgabat in late October 1996 for more than a month. The incident occured soon after Durdyev published an article criticising Turkmenistan in the Russian paper *Pravda*. He was released in late

November in poor condition. Since his incarceration, Durdyev has reportedly been dismissed from the editorial boards of the publications with which he was associated as well as from his teaching positions. His membership of the Academy of Science has also reportedly been revoked. (CPJ)

## UGANDA

In an interview in a local paper on 8 December 1996 John Nagenda, public relations and media advisor to President Yoweri Museveni, threatened a government crackdown on 'negative reporting' on the war in the north of the country. (Uganda Journalist Safety Committee, West Africa)

Freelance journalist **Muasazi-Namiti** was arrested on 26 January and charged with seditious libel in connection with two articles published in the *Crusader* on 23 January and *Secrets* magazine on 30 January. The articles detailed the sexual exploits of Hassan Kato, who claims to have slept with 1,000 women. Kato was also arrested on 22 January on the same charge. Muasazi-Namiti was released the same day on bail. (CPJ)

## UKRAINE

On 7 January that the eastern region of Kharkiv voted to give the Russian language equal status with Ukrainian. However, the Russian-speaking eastern region of Donetsk decided that the official administrative and business languages should be solely

Ukrainian. The Constitution stipulates that Ukrainian is the official state language, but in regions with sizeable minorities, other languages can be granted official status. (OMRI)

It was reported on 8 January that an article in the Chernigov local paper, *Trudovaya Slava*, entitled 'Seen and Experienced', was stopped because of 'understatement and underevaluation of the role of the Communist party of the USSR in the victory over fascism'. It was also reported that if the author, **Vasily Kritsky**, stops working with newspapers published by the organisation Popular Rukh of Ukraine, the article may be published. (*Express Khronika*)

## UNITED KINGDOM

On 17 December 1996 the Appeal Court upheld the Radio Authority's ban on broadcast advertisements by **Amnesty International UK** (AIUK), issued in May 1994 (*Index* 4/1995). (AI)

On 18 December Brian Basham, former head of public relations for British Airways, was granted an injunction preventing further distribution of the book *Dirty Tricks* by journalist **Martyn Gregory** (see *Index* 1/1997). He also won damages of US$35,000 plus costs. The book alleged Basham had orchestrated a smear campaign against Virgin Atlantic Airways in 1991. (*Guardian*)

In a landmark decision on 20 December the High Court

ruled that a blanket ban on journalists interviewing inmates in prison was illegal and an unjustified restriction on freedom of speech. The ruling followed test cases brought by two prisoners, Ian Simms and Michael O'Brien, whose life sentences for murder were being investigated as possible cases of miscarriages of justice by freelance journalist **Bob Woffinden** and BBC Wales reporter **Karen Voisey** respectively. Both journalists had refused to sign undertakings not to publish any material obained during prison visits. (*Guardian*)

Eight out of 10 local branches of Waterstone's and WH Smith's book stores refused to stock a biography of the controversial comedian Bernard Manning by Jonathan Margolis in January, leading to accusations of censorship. (*Guardian*)

Clauses contained in the government's Social Security Administration (Fraud) Bill passing through Parliament in January would enable civil servants to engage in 'data matching' without the knowledge or consent of the individuals concerned. The bill allows information held by Inland Revenue, Customs and Excise or the Home Office to be disclosed to the Department of Social Security (DSS) in order to prevent, detect, investigate or prosecute offences relating to social security. The absence of a statutory code to control the activities of civil servants involved in matching personal data was criticised by the Data Protection Registrar,

while Justice, the British arm of the International Commission of Jurists, said the bill was 'an unprecedented extension of the powers of the secretary of state and local authorities to share information on individuals'. (*Guardian*)

One letter bomb exploded injuring two employees and three further bombs were discovered at the London offices of the leading Arab newspaper *al-Hayat* on 14 January. They are thought to be linked to eight other bombs sent to *al-Hayat* offices in the USA between 31 December 1996 and 3 January, following an editorial in the paper strongly critical of Islamist terrorism. (*Financial Times*)

The government was defeated on 20 January in the House of Lords at the report stage of the Police Bill, over its proposals to allow police to 'bug and burgle' homes and offices without prior judicial authorisation (*Index* 1/1997). At the bill's third reading in the Lords on 28 January, the government narrowly won the vote against Labour's calls for an amendment designed to protect solicitors' offices from bugging operations. On 11 February the home secretary, Michael Howard, announced an amendment to the bill, conceding that the planting of police surveillance devices in homes, offices, hotel bedrooms and the offices of lawyers, doctors and journalists, should require prior authorisation by government-appointed surveillance commissioners, except in emergencies. Civil liberties groups and lawyers remain concerned about the privacy threat and said the police should be required to get prior authority from senior judges. (*Independent, Financial Times, Guardian*)

On 24 January a High Court judgement ruled that, under the offence of trespassory assembly aimed at curbing protests on public roads, police can ban groups of 20 or more meeting in a particular area if they fear 'serious disruption to the life of the community', even if the meeting is non-obstructive and non-violent. The judgement related to the cases of Margaret Jones and Richard Lloyd, who were the first to be convicted of trespassory assembly under the 1994 Criminal Justice Act after taking part in a peaceful demonstration at Stonehenge in 1995. (*Guardian, Times*)

The newsagent chain W H Smith announced on 12 February that it was to withdraw soft-porn magazines *Penthouse, For Women, Playboy* and *Mayfair* from all its shops except those at railway stations and airports from March. The chain denied charges of censorship and claimed the move was a response to falling demand. (*Guardian, Independent*)

The government suffered a defeat over the Jurisdiction (Conspiracy and Incitement) Bill on 14 February. The private member's bill would have made it a criminal act to incite or organise acts in a foreign country that are ille-

gal both there and in Britain, and includes as a form of incitement the communication of 'messages' from Britain to opposition groups abroad. Civil liberties groups are concerned that such legislation could have been used against political refugees fighting for justice in their own countries. (*Guardian*)

## URUGUAY

**Pablo Alfano**, a journalist with the Montevideo daily *El Observador*, was kidnapped by two people on 28 January. They drove him around in a car for half an hour while attempting to discover the sources of an investigation Alfano is working on by offering him money and threatening both him and his family. They also warned him against continuing his work. (IAPA)

## USA

Satirical writer and filmmaker **Michael Moore** has been banned from the Borders bookshop chain following his support for striking workers outside a Borders shop where he was due to sign copies of his book *Downsize This! Random Threats from an Unarmed American*. Moore's support for former Borders employee Miriam Fried, sacked for her union activities, led to the nationwide ban. Moore is donating a proportion of the royalties from his book to support the striking workers. (*Nation*)

The Parental Choice in Television Programming,

which seeks to regulate viewing through an age-based ratings system and use of the v-chip (*Index* 2/1996) came into effect in January. The system will run for a 10-month trial period. It divides into six categories ranging from TVY, suitable for children of all ages; TVY7, suitable for children of seven years and older; TVPG, where parental guidance is suggested; TV14, suitable for children of 14 or over; and TVM, for mature audiences. The appropriate classification will be displayed in the corner of the screen for all programmes other than news and sport. At the end of February the new system came in for criticism from politicians from both major parties, who would prefer ratings to be based on content. The television industry has vowed to fight any such development. (Reuters)

On 23 January a New York court ruled that the 1996 **Military Honor and Decency Act** (*Index* 6/1996), which restricts the sale of pornography on military bases, is unconstitutional. (Reuters)

On 12 February Mississippi state governor Kirk Fordice signed into law a ban on same-sex marriages, making his state the 28th to go on record against the practice. The flurry of state laws against gay marriage has been prompted by the possibility that courts in Hawaii might legalise them. A Honolulu district court is currently considering an appeal by a gay couple who argue that nonrecognition of same-sex marriages constitutes an infringement of their civil rights. (Reuters)

The Supreme Court ruled on 19 February that restrictions that say anti-abortion protesters must keep 15 feet away from women or cars visiting abortion clinics in upstate New York constitute an impermissibly vague restriction on freedom of speech. However, the court also ruled that a fixed 15-foot exclusion zone around a clinic's entrance and driveway is a legitimate restriction on freedom of expression. (Reuters)

New York City lawyers filed an appeal with the Supreme Court on 26 February, challenging a Federal Appeals Court ruling granting First Amendment protection to artists who sell their work on the city's streets. City authorities want to impose a licensing system on street artists. (Artists' Response To Illegal State Tactics)

Thirteen commentaries by **Mumia Abu-Jamal** (*Index* 1/1997) which were scheduled for broadcast on a dozen Pennsylvania radio stations between 24 February and 8 March were cancelled at the last minute. The commentaries were due to go out on the daily political talk show 'Democracy Now!'. The interviews were recorded by the Prison Radio Project in October 1996, shortly before the Pennsylvania Department of Corrections banned all journalists from its prisons in what has been called the

'Mumia rule' (*Index* 1/1996). (Equal Justice)

### UZBEKISTAN

The state-owned media published a call by President Islam Karimov for greater freedom of information at the end of 1996. However, few believe that this signals an end to tight media curbs in the former Soviet republic. Karimov, a former Communist party chief, said that stronger democratic institutions and greater protection of human rights should be guaranteed in the central Asian republic. 'Promoting a democratic press will be the third direction of political reform,' he said. (Reuters)

### VENEZUELA

On 23 January journalist **William Ojeda** (see page 104) began his 14-month prison sentence in El Junquito prison. Convicted in December 1996, he was charged with defamation in his book *How Much is a Judge Worth?*, in which he named a number of judges and magistrates with links to the government, powerful business interests and organised crime. Ojeda is able to appeal but all legal avenues lead to the Supreme Court, the majority of which is composed of the same judges accused in the book. Ojeda and his lawyers are thus appealing directly to the president. (FIP)

### VIETNAM

Strict new state controls to

combat the effects of the country's rapid economic growth and open-door policies were reported in late January. They include tighter screening of applications for exit visas and passports, stricter controls on imported periodicals, 10 days' compulsory labour each year for all between the ages of 18 and 45, mandatory purchase and reading of the official newspaper *Nhan Dan* by party cells, branches and mass organisations, and the creation of party cells in all foreign firms and organisations. In addition, the official Vietnam Buddhist Church was instructed to strive for 'closer Buddhist solidarity and national unity' in response to criticism of the government's approach to religion from abroad. (*South China Morning Post*, Reuters)

### ZAIRE

**Emmanuel Katshunga**, a journalist with the independent paper *La Tempête des Tropiques*, was arrested at the paper's offices by state security agents on 20 January. The arrest was in connection with an article Katshunga had written about a branch of the military which is known as the President's Special Division. (CPJ, RSF)

Freelance journalist **Jean Mbenga Muagianvita** has been held incommunicado in Kinshasa since his arrest by the Military Action and Intelligence Service (SARM) on 23 January in connection with a series of articles he wrote about President Mobutu's American-based

• • • • • • • • • • • • • • • • • • • • • • • • • • • • • • • •

## WILLIAM OJEDA

# How much is a judge worth?

This book was originally inspired by an investigation that I began in 1991 into the Colombian drug trade. I concluded that the country's weak and corrupt institutions had given the trade its power to permeate society, to the extent of becoming a parallel government. On my return to Venezuela, however, I realised that the social decay occurring in Colombia was also taking place here — through the destruction of our judicial system. My fears now switch constantly between the chaos and deficiencies within this system and the effect its vulnerability has on the consolidation of criminal activities such as drug trafficking in our country...

...The Venezuelan judicial system has terminal cancer. Its entire infrastructure is atrophied by party politics, mediocrity and corruption. The distribution of jobs either by appointment or through rigged exams is part of a chain reaction that has its inception in the 'Fixed Point' agreement. Through this, two or three political parties share and alternate power equally between themselves at every level of the hierarchy.

A body suffering from cancer must amputate the part that cannot be cured. In the same way, many of those who have infiltrated the administration of the national judicial system need to be extricated. No suitable instrument exists, however, to cut out the malignant cells: the law guarantees that judges are untouchable and the Judicial Council has virtually no effective legal mechanisms at their disposal for such an operation.

The judicial hierarchy is being eaten away by corruption at every level: among the clerks and secretaries at the bottom; the judges in the middle; and the magistrates of the judiciary, the Superior Tribunal and the Supreme Court of Justice at the top. None of them act in the interests of the people: none are

political lobbyists. SARM is refusing to produce him in court until he reveals his sources. Muagianvita's 14-year-old daughter was raped by soldiers after a search of his home. (CPJ)

Opposition politician **Joseph Oligankoye** fled to Brazzaville, Congo, on 16 February after the Zairean government ordered the arrest of the organisers of a civil disobedience day on 10 February. The protesters called for people to reject new money put into circulation by the Bank of Zaire. Following the action, private television and radio stations have been banned by the government from broadcasting political programmes, including newscasts and press reviews. (SWB)

Recent publication: *Hidden from Scrutiny — Human Rights Abuses in Eastern Zaire* (AI, December 1996, 11pp)

President Chiluba suspended High Court judge **Kabazo**

motivated solely by the fulfilment of their duty. It goes without saying that the Supreme Court of Justice has no independent sanctioning body. They pay themselves and they give themselves the change; thus not one of their magistrates has ever been or ever will be held accountable. On the contrary, they are all free to negotiate their own deals. Driven by the desire to satisfy their appetite, they rapidly become insatiable.

Many of the problems of the judicial system are due to the lack of professional training among magistrates. More than 50 per cent of the judges studied at universities of 'doubtful reputation' and more than 60 per cent have an extremely poor academic record. As a result, they resort to immorality and vice as a means of survival.

Greed and complicity rule from the lowest clerks to the Magistrate of the Judicial Council. No-one tells on anyone else. We are all accomplices in a system where shamelessness is 'legal'. If one person is courageous enough to challenge it, defence mechanisms and solidarity immediately come into play to silence or destroy the accuser.

If some member of our judicial system decides not to fall in with a dishonest act as a result of reading this text, then all the time, risk, effort and hard work that has gone into creating it will be justified. For it was written in the hope that one day we might have justice through a system protected by the accusing finger of a society tired of impunity and tired of its impotence in the face of abusive power: a society that has too often been tempted to take the law into its own hands.

*Excerpted from ¿Cuánto Vale un Juez? (How Much is a Judge Worth?) by William Ojeda, published by Vadell Hermanos, Caracas, 1996*

*Translated by Emily Walmsley*

● ● ● ● ● ● ● ● ● ● ● ● ● ● ● ● ● ● ● ● ● ● ● ● ● ● ● ● ● ● ●

**Chanda** in mid-January and ordered an investigation into his conduct. Given Chanda's outspokenness on the country's human rights record, many in the judiciary and opposition parties believe the suspension to be political. Judge Chanda overruled the speaker of Parliament, Robinson Nabulyato, who had sentenced Fred M'membe and Bright Mwape of the *Post* to indefinite prison terms for contempt of Parliament (*Index* 3/1996, 4/1996). (*Mail & Guardian*)

**Kunda Mwila**, a reporter for the *Post*, was arrested on 22 January and detained for four hours for 'conduct likely to cause a breach of the peace'. Mwila was arrested in appar-ent retaliation for exposing a plainclothes policeman, Innocent Kanunga, who had claimed to be a journalist on the *Chronicle* newspaper at a press conference. (MISA, *Post*)

On 28 January an injunction preventing the broadcast of the programme 'A Trail of Deceit' on ZNBC-TV was lifted. The film deals with an alleged conspiracy between the opposition United National Independence Party (UNIP) and the *Post* newspaper to influence donors to freeze aid to the country. (MISA)

The deputy president, Godfrey Miyanda, told Parliament on 6 February that the government plans to censor 'dirty programmes' displaying nudity on ZNBC-TV, because they run contrary to Christian values and are screened too close to Christian programmes. (MISA)

On 6 February Ernest Mwansa, deputy minister of information and broadcasting services, dismissed concerns of media workers that government plans to establish a Media Council of Zambia (MCZ), announced on 17 January, would limit press freedom. He also accused Zambian journalists working for foreign media of distorting information for the sake of 'a few dollars'. (MISA)

**Masautso Phiri**, special projects editor of the *Post*, was gaoled by the Supreme Court for three months on 11 February. He was found guilty of contempt of court for writing an article entitled 'Praising God Loudly', which alleged that the seven Supreme Court judges had been paid a total of US$5 million to rule against a challenge by opposition parties to the candidacy of President Chiluba in the 18 November elections. In passing sentence, deputy chief justice

Bonaventure Bweupe said 'only a short prison sentence would send such a shock wave to the accused and others with a like mind'. (MISA)

**Lweeno Hamusankwa**, editor of the *Chronicle*, was arrested on 16 February in Lusaka and charged with criminal libel and 'publishing false news with intent to cause fear and alarm to the public'. The charge arose from articles which alleged that arms and ammunition had been stolen from Mikongo Barracks in Lusaka, and another which accused a presidential aide of using a stolen vehicle. He was released on bail on 18 February. (MISA, *Post*)

### ZIMBABWE

The independent monthly magazine **Horizon** was charged with defamation on 27 November 1996 in connection with an article published in October 1991, which alleged that former army commander General Solomon Mujuru had been 'dishonest' in his business dealings. Mujuru was awarded US$4,000 in damages. The magazine is to appeal. (MISA)

★★★

General publications: *Great Lakes — Repatriation, Refoulement and the Safety of Refugees and the Internally Displaced* (AI, 24 January 1997, 13pp); *Against the Tide — The Death Penalty in Southeast Asia* (AI, January

1997, 25pp); *World Press Freedom Review 1996* (International Press Institute, January 1997, 107pp); *African Conflict and the Media* by Abiodun Onadipe and David Lord (Conciliation Resources, 1997, 25pp)

★★★

*Compiled by: Penny Dale (Africa); Nicholas McAulay, Mansoor Mirza, Sarah Smith (Asia); Ann Chambers, Vera Rich (eastern Europe & CIS); Emily Walmsley (Latin America); Michaela Becker, Philippa Nugent (Middle East); Briony Stocker (north America & Pacific); Rose Bell (western Europe)*

## ASSOCIATION FOR THE STUDY OF ETHNICITY AND NATIONALISM

### IS PLEASED TO ANNOUNCE ITS SEVENTH ANNUAL CONFERENCE

# NATIONALISM AND DEMOCRACY

### Friday 18 April 1997
### London School of Economics and Political Science
### London, UK

Speakers: Michael Mann, David Miller, John Schwarzmantel, Sammy Smooha, Yael Tamir and David Welsh

Since its foundation in 1990 ASEN has established an international and multidisciplinary network of scholars interested in ethnicity and nationalism. Through its conferences, seminars and publications ASEN provides a forum for debate and discussion of issues concerning ethnicity and nationalism in all areas of the world.

In addition to the Annual Conference, ASEN's activities include:

*   Publication of **Nations and Nationalism**, the leading scholarly journal devoted to the study of nationalism (Cambridge University Press)
*   Publication of the **ASEN Bulletin**, a biannual extended newsletter for ASEN members
*   Organisation of seminars and lectures

**For information about the Conference and/or ASEN, contact:**
**ASEN, Room H659, London School of Economics,**
**Houghton Street, London WC2 2AE**
**Tel: 0171 955 6801, Fax: 0171 955 6218**
**E-mail: ASEN@LSE.AC.UK**

# Looking
# at kids

**The first near universally ratified human rights treaty in history, boasts the UN, yet the UN Convention on the Rights of the Child is, says Caroline Moorehead, 'all something of a sham'. Almost everything it promised to remedy has got worse, from child labour and prostitution in the developing world to the vacuous and uncaring world inhabited by the child victims of the collapse of Communism. In the West, the 'crisis in the family' encompasses the demolition of the once caring state and revelations of domestic child abuse. What have we done to our children? How do we see them? What do we hear from them?**

*Britain 1990s: Gypsy children play amid the garbage Credit: Vicky White/Photofusion*

# IRENA MARYNIAK

# Whatever happened to Soviet childhood?

**The state of Russia's children provides a metaphor for the collapse of the Communist dream**

*'We shall prove to them that they are mere pitiable children, but that the happiness of a child is the sweetest of all. We shall make their life like a children's game, with children's songs, in chorus, and with innocent dances... it will relieve them of their present terrible torments of coming to a free decision themselves. And they will all be happy...thousands of millions of happy infants...' Fyodor Dostoyevsky,* The Brothers Karamazov, 1880

ONCE upon a time, there was a boy, and his name was Vitya. He had short spiky hair, bright little eyes and a cheeky grin and he was just 13. Vitya lived in a sprawling, troubled metropolis about 1,000 miles west of the Urals. Every morning he would get up and hurry off to the Dinamo metro station where, in between mooching and pilfering and very possibly other things, he did odd jobs carting boxes for the equivalent of about a dollar a day. And every night he would scramble up to the sixth floor of one of those looming grey apartment blocks to see his brothers and sisters and, of course, his mother and give her what he had earned: which was nice for her because she badly needed a tipple every now and again. After that he would go home. Vitya lived in a kennel. This wasn't too bad because there was a dog in the kennel who got a fistful of scraps every day which he shared with Vitya. But then it was December and Vitya's feet froze.

One day a beer-cart driver called Anatoly saw Vitya at the Dinamo station and stopped off for a chinwag. He wanted to know Vitya's name and where he lived and why he was having such trouble shifting those boxes. The next day Anatoly brought some friends and they examined Vitya's feet. And because this is a tale for those who long for happy ends, they all turned out to be from the Leopold Union for the Protection of Orphans, and they drove Vitya off to a sanatorium where his feet could be treated. Anatoly took Vitya home to his wife and three children, and they fostered him for a year. They also tried to teach him to read. After that, the Leopold Union arranged for Vitya and his four brothers and sisters to be placed in a children's home on Garibaldi Street in the southwest corner of the city. And they all lived happily ever after.

If statistics and press reports are any more a reflection of the true state of things than stories told over a glass of *Pickwick* tea in a Moscow bar, Vitya could have known worse. He might have been picked up for slave labour in Azerbaijan where, *Argumenty i Fakty* reports, children are kept as unpaid house servants by well-heeled families with an image to think about. He might have slipped into drug smuggling or prostitution, or ended up fruit-picking in an isolated settlement in the central Asian outback where children are said to work for 14-16 hours a day under armed guard. Or he might have been sold to the West, either for adoption or, as lurid Moscow tabloids claim, as an organ donor.

In fact, Vitya was taken into care by one of those private child-welfare charities which have been springing up in Russia over the past five years, in response to the soaring numbers of children on the streets and to the harsh reputation of overcrowded state orphanages remaining from Soviet times. With their impenetrable concrete walls, collective regimentation and corrupt administrations, supporters of the new voluntary sector say, they leave their inmates dependent, stultified and spectacularly unprepared for assimilation into a market community. But of the more than 300 independent children's charities active in Moscow now, many are run on enthusiasm rather than professional skill and some operate well outside the law. Others are downright nefarious.

One of the most reputable is NAN (No to Alcoholism and Drugs), which runs a children's shelter in a northern Moscow suburb, encased by apartment blocks and a small patch of woodland. It's called 'The Way Home'. I approached it after dark, guided only by a neon searchlight dazzlingly poised on the roof. The compound had thick metal railings and, as it turned out, two very locked gates. Hard to tell whether this was intended to keep strangers out or children in. I circled the grounds, tramping through viscous mud and peering anxiously for a footpath through the trees. There was none. In daylight, doubtless, it would have been innocuous enough. After an oddly timeless space I caught sight of a stooped figure shuffling between the birches a little way ahead.

The old woman (Russia breeds old and young, with little in between) was unperturbed to be approached by a breathless and visibly unsettled foreigner. She explained insistently and at length that this really wasn't the way things used to be. Only a year or two ago *anyone* could get in. But now we were back at the main gate and, somehow, somebody from inside the building must have seen us. An anonymous-looking figure in plain clothes emerged and, once assured that I had an appointment, opened up. My guide was left waving on the other side of the barrier.

Inside it was warm, kindly and very clean. Before visiting the children's dormitories I was asked, in the nicest possible way, to remove those mud-caked boots. Here, Sapar Koulyanov, the director, is surrogate father to about 30 children aged three to 13. It was 8pm on a Wednesday; party-time in the directors' study. There was tea and biscuits and music and dancing, and as a special treat Sapar took photographs of everyone with his Polaroid camera. It was all very reassuringly normal. Each child had a history a bit like Vitya's, but here everyone was fed and clothed and out of danger, at least for the moment. The regime was relaxed and benignly paternalistic.

Sapar Mullaevich talks about the present with a kind of suppressed horror and about the past with ill-concealed nostalgia: cosy little backyards between apartment blocks where children could play in safety; Palaces of Culture where any hobby was catered for after school hours — athletics, drama, music, airplane modelling; secure schooling with the certainty of work at the other end; those long sun-splashed summers in Pioneer camps and the neatly coiffed little girls with huge bows in their hair.

'It all seems to be about money and prestige these days,' he says tentatively and his voice is an unbroken sigh. 'There may seem to be a bubbling universal freedom, in which everything is permitted but then, on the other hand, one has to pause. One may even be tempted to think that this is wrong, that there should, after all, be a collective morality.'

In a sense 'The Way Home', so pristine, easygoing and cheerful, was like a projection of the world many former Soviet citizens must hanker

*Young pioneer camp in Soviet Crimea 1930s: 'Let the sun shine forever, Let there always be me'*
*Credit: Society for Cooperation in Russian & Soviet Studies*

for. Barred, protected from the outside, warm and welcoming within; a place where immediate needs are met and socialising codes of conduct taught. Here, if anywhere in modern Russia, children will learn something of the old Soviet values instilled in their carers by the Pioneer movement and the Komsomol: respect for authority, diligence, obedience, good manners, helpfulness and, by extension, docility, conformity and an ambition confined to a diploma, an apartment, a job, a family, perhaps a car. All costly commodities these days. Perhaps by some kind of osmosis they will get a whiff, too, of those golden days when morality meant devotion to the Spiritual Father of the Nation (as Stalin liked to be known) before loyalty to blood kinship. And that may be something that *these* young people — neglected or abandoned by their closest kith and kin — will more easily understand than most.

THERE was a Pioneer in those golden days whose name was Pavlik Morozov. He lived in a village in the Urals and he wore a white shirt and a blazing red scarf. When he was 13 he stood up under Lenin's portrait before the local governing council and denounced his father for collaboration with the *kulaks*. It was 1932. His story became the myth on which all Soviet children were raised because, shortly afterwards, he was murdered. He became the model to which all Pioneers were to aspire, the archetype they were to reflect as they performed their countless salutes, their missions and assignments, received badges and prizes for good behaviour, celebrated feast-days in memory of Soviet heroes, and sang in unison around the camp fire:

*Let the sun shine forever*
*Let the sky always be*
*Let there always be mama*
*Let there always be me.*

Later there would be the Komsomol, harvesting brigades, summer construction camps: the Komsomol City-on-the-Amur, Magnet City in the Urals, the Bailkal-Amur Railway... Trailblazing projects all, built by Communist Youth, their tents pitched on mountains and steppes and riversides. No sex, fights or drugs, just the power of faith, enthusiasm and hard work — or so the subsidised hoopla which surrounded them would have had us believe.

That was before jazz, gays, drugs and bourgeois eroticism came muscling in. The only discordant notes in this glorious chorale were the itinerant kids who would appear in well-heeled resorts, sometimes armed, and claim to be implementing social justice by fleecing the better off. They were the neglected children of the post-revolutionary decades — victims of combat, hunger and relocation — who poured into cities, flooded train stations and markets and derelict houses and could be found packed into the undercarriages of trains on the way to holiday resorts in the Crimea. They terrorised their peers, dismayed or infuriated adults and deeply embarrassed successive regimes by surviving burrowed into woodpiles, haystacks, coal reserves, drainage pipes, garbage dumps and cemetery burial vaults.

The summer of 1917 left 150,000 children destitute in Petrograd alone. But the economic and political transition of the 1990s, war in the former republics, the migration of refugees and the relocation of the military have deposited a legacy hardly less devastating. What statistics there are indicate that in democratic Russia up to 700,000 children are on the streets; over 400,000 are known to be orphaned; around 30,000 are listed as disappeared; and 150,000 run away from home every year. None of these figures take account of the war in Chechnya.

According to *Moscow News* correspondent Galina Mashtakova, countless children now fend for themselves in the cellars and shattered apartment blocks of Grozny. They dart about in oversize ladies' sweaters and newly acquired green velvet berets begging, pilfering and sniffing glue. During the war they had the job of cycling round the city to check out the numbers of Russian Federal troops, their position and ammunition stores. These days they rummage for unused shells in the cellars and snowdrifts of Grozny and sell them to Chechen fighters for the equivalent of US$6 apiece. Those living alone in relatively undamaged property are exposed to danger from racketeers, and from the desperate, on the prowl for living space. Two adolescent orphans Mashtakova befriended last October were murdered a month later in exactly these circumstances.

But the hundreds of thousands of kids roaming Russian cities — diving past you into the Moscow metro, whooping gleefully as they release yet another dog some hapless owner has left tied to a tree — are, more often than not, merely preferring the questionable allure of the streets to abuse, violence and dipsomania at home. Though after a scheme for the

# Alyosha's story

The first thing was that my mum lost me at the station. Then me and my friend from the station we went off to the airport at Bykovo. At the airport we got caught and they took us off to the allocation centre. Then they took me back to my dad. My mum and dad got divorced. I was five then. Yeah...anyway they got divorced. So I ran away from my dad. I ran away because I didn't want to live there. He got married again. I ran away and then I got caught and I ran away from him a few times after that. Then they sent me here.

You want to know what it was like on the streets? Well, I got to know this boy, Sashka. We used to scrounge off people and he knew how to nick things. He had a brother. But it was the two of us. We went off to the GUM, the department store, with this brother or cousin of his. But before that we played on fruit machines and slept under the stairs and in attics. We used to get money off people. You go up to them, you're skint, and they give it you. Some people gave five, and some 50 [roubles]. I got 20,000 once. And once I found 5,000. But that was before I got to know Sashka under the stairs. Then we got to know one another and we slept in the attic and smoked.

I still smoke, but they don't have fags here.

Then I got to know this other boy, Leshka. And I lived with him in his flat. They did deals there. His mum did. She had this friend, a good friend. Azerbaijani... or Ukrainian, I can't remember now. Maybe he was Ukrainian. He laughed a lot.

Leshka and me, we did a lot together. It was good. We'd get 50, or maybe 20, I'm not sure. And we drank all this wine. We drank and got pissed. On the second day we had champagne, and on the third day... They had a good time there with vodka, *Moskovskaya*, the Russian sort. They used to have these bottles, you know, the really big ones you can buy. And we'd drink with Leshka. And get drunk.

We slept up in the attic. It wasn't that cold really. There were blankets, and they stuck paper on the walls. We had this friend who lived at home. He was big, 13.

So we went off to the GUM and my friend got caught. Then I managed to get 1,000. Well...no... First of all I went to the Paveletskaya station to take a look round. It wasn't that really, I stayed there all the time. I knew there were these automatic gates in the hall. The police bring them down and that's it. You can't get out. Except you can, but only if you know how. Then you can run away.

I never nicked things, but my friend did. He got 45,000 out of a pocket once, just like that. I can do it too. But I never did. (Except once. But that's a secret.)

*St Petersburg, Russia 1990s: children of the streets*

One night I took 500 roubles off a policeman. But I don't know if he was a policeman really. They beat me up. And then he said: 'Right. We're going to the militia.' But I ran away. I wriggled and fought and went tearing off.

I was out there for three months. My dad, he just drank a lot, that's why I ran away. But my friend's dad, he took injections. I saw him do it once. They can put you in prison for drugs.

Now I'm here. I've started school. They've given me clothes. There's the circus. It's pretty good really. The other day they took us to see all these weapons the Samurai used. The Americans dropped a nuclear bomb on Hiroshima and Nagasaki. And we fought in World War II too. One of the bombs was called 'Little Boy'. And I can't remember the name of the other.

*Alyosha is 11 and currently lives at the NAN childrens' shelter in Moscow. He spoke to Irena Maryniak* privatisation of apartments was introduced after 1991, some parents reportedly sold up and made off, leaving an estimated 100,000 children to fend for themselves.

They shelter mostly in the attics of tenement blocks and in cellars, at railway stations and airports, in small groups with a teenage leader who acts as financial manager, housing adviser, judge and agent of punishment. Some wash cars. Some get caught up in organised crime. According to the Charities Aid Foundation, adolescent professional killers are sometimes willing to do the job for as little as 100,000 roubles (less than US$20).

It is a chilling sign of the times. But then eight out of 10 families in Russia live below the poverty line. Education, career prospects and entertainment are reserved for the privileged few. The rest are relegated to the stairwells, out of the way of parents weighed down by job losses, inflation and personal distress. A recent report in *Izvestiya*, from the Kemerovskaya region in the Urals, depicted an entire community centred around the town refuse dump which also serves as a refuge for growing numbers of scavenging kids who shelter at night in the heating plant chimney. With pay packages months overdue, the sale of discarded bottles is a surer source of income than working down a mine shaft. And they are here for the taking beside piles of decaying garbage of all kinds and, just occasionally, the body of a new-born child.

The economic transition of eastern Europe has placed the very young at the epicentre of a seismic shift. Where poverty and crime has risen they have been its chief victims. For underworld networks, drugsmugglers and paedophiles, the map of Europe and Asia has been redrawn. The collapse of the Soviet Empire opened new supply routes for drugs from Pakistan and Afghanistan via Russia and the new independent states, and aided the proliferation of smuggling rings from Tallinn to Rangoon. These days drugs are sold by old ladies outside the Lubianka (once the KGB headquarters) to addicts and to kids. The collapse of the Berlin Wall has drawn paedophiles to the banks of the Danube and to public spots in Warsaw or Prague. Teenagers from Ukraine or Romania appear in the cities of central Europe for a spell of prostitution and subsequently vanish. The tales Russian street children tell of violence, sexual harassment or arbitrary detention find easy echo in Bucharest, Budapest or, as a recent Human Rights Watch report on police brutality against the children of Bulgaria amply documents, in Sofia.

In the early 1980s, Gabor Demszky was an underground publisher and founder of SZETA, the first independent social welfare organisation in Hungary. Subsequently he spent six months in prison and today he is mayor of Budapest. He elaborates conscientiously on rationalisation of expenditure and public transport problems, and only when pressed begins to speak of attitudes that characterise the economically polarised societies of central and eastern Europe: inadequate social and economic mobility, lack of tolerance, raging competition and inflexibility. 'Young professionals, talented people make fortunes, but they don't understand the problems of the rest,' he announces with sudden animation. 'In this yuppie subculture, there isn't much social feeling, solidarity, or sensitivity. This is also true of the new bourgeoisie. There is absolutely no openness and no understanding of social tensions.' The same is true of the 'new Russian' social and political culture, with the Kremlin still, as ever, nominating the winners and consigning its losers to limbo.

Statistics acknowledge that between 1992 and 1994 child crime more than doubled in Russia. Young offenders are left to await trial for up to three years in Interior Ministry investigation cells built for four inmates and shared by up to 15. There is seldom opportunity to exercise; violence, rape and murder are rife because prison guards prefer not to intervene in disputes between prisoners. An arbitrary decision by a prison guard can have a 15-year-old stripped and despatched to an unheated isolation cell with no light and a soaking floor for between five and 10 days. Later, if convicted, adolescents have to endure educational labour colonies ruled less by official administrators than by internal hierarchies in which inmates are classified within their own community as masters, lackeys or slaves according to strength, wit and will. 'Slavery', of course, implies routine taunts, humiliation and rape.

The investigation cells and educational labour colony are as much of an insult to east European democracy today as labour camps were to the original Communist Utopia. To children without family relationships, a community or a welfare state to help give shape to the world, democratisation has offered a vacuous universe with neither order nor rationale. Deprived of cultural or educational grounding, and of any credible political, economic or social point of reference, the unwanted children of eastern Europe live on a plane of shifting sands. And who, after all, would dare to blame them if, one day, they come to elect a life 'in chorus' which will relieve them at last of their present terrible torment of coming to a free decision themselves? ❑

● ● ● ● ● ● ● ● ● ● ● ● ● ● ● ● ● ● ● ● ● ● ● ● ● ● ● ● ●

# Hungarian Gruftis

GABOR DETTRE

*'Gruftis have a kind of primitive rule — I don't know who invented it, I think some Hungarian — that they either die when they're 17 or when they're 23. The one they called 'Little Grufti' committed suicide because he was 17' (Red-haired girl)*

*Girl with blond, bushy hair shaved at the sides and wearing black make-up:*

I had this boyfriend who I trusted a lot. And one day he just said: 'There is another girl and that's it. It's finished.' I am sad for my parents too. They are sick, and they have three young children. Often I go to sleep and I think 'I never want to wake up again.' This is because I can't bear to see my parents, and sisters and brothers suffer. I have this little brother: who knows what will happen when he grows up? He will also be disappointed in life. That is very bad.

There is a cold wind blowing underneath me
I hold my cold desires in the eternal wrinkles of my face
And I am gathering companions against an ever-greying world
Part of a small team: me and my pencil
We sit — the two of us — in the cold winter night
I create my dreams which will crumble in two days
I mend them, they revive but sadly disintegrate
Bitter moon, my old friend, you are sweating
Why is your scarred face looking at me?
Do you still see properly?...

The days go by. The years go by. I've changed. I live differently. I only trust myself. I don't believe in anyone else.

Then came the 'Domal'. You have to inhale it. Then came the pills. Then the wrist cutting. My relationship broke down with my parents at that time too. I turned away from them. I was only interested in my friends. They took me to a hospital because of the Domal — that's a drug. You can buy it in any household shop. It costs two [Hungarian] Forints and 50 Fillers (a few cents). It's a stain remover. Then I tried inhaling a penetrating spray and glue but they weren't as strong. Now Domal has been banned.

I just exist from day to day. I don't know what will happen to me. I would like to work. I've always wanted to help sick people or little children. I've always wanted to work with the mentally handicapped. I've been to a home for the handicapped several times, and I've seen how they treat people there — like animals. That's why I would like to work in a place like this. I have more feeling than the nurses who are already there. But to do this you need an education which I don't have.

*Brown-haired girl with long bangs:*

I await death with a strange kind of calm. Death is eternal peace. A place where a person no longer feels pain, although it is a place where you won't feel happiness either. But in our lives there is a lot more pain than happiness.

*From* Tomorrow is Cancelled due to Lack of Interest, *a documentary made by Hungarian film-maker Gabor Dettre. The blonde girl and the red-head have both committed suicide since the film was made*

• • • • • • • • • • • • • • • • • • • • • • • • • • • • • • • • • • • •

# MARIAN ALLSOPP

# A triptych for our times

**Children, victims as well as villains, are the symbol of an uncertain future. There is a crisis in the family but we have not found a different way of living together, a new definition of family in which all its members can feel safe and cared for**

NEVER before have children and images of childhood had such symbolic force in adult debate. Their pictures are like banners carried into war in a struggle over how best to order our social and economic relations: children, parents, families, industries, communities and the state. Our modern media stars — Jamie Bulger, the Dunblane children, Rikki Neave — peer out of their newsprint frames like the denizens of some endangered species, their mute appeal more powerful than a million words. They are the guarantors of authenticity in our arguments; they legitimate competing claims and give force to our rhetoric.

And here I hope to use these images in the same way — as a vivid shorthand for a complex story about social change. This story is not about childhood as such, though children are implicated as much as any other social group. But I do not see childhood, bounded though it is in language and legislation and by our desire to protect it, as a separate state. The more, it seems, that adults mark the difference, the more they are afraid they are the same.

Marina Warner, in her elegant Reith lectures of 1994, showed that children have always had a special place in western iconography just *because* they represent 'essential humanity'. Not only are they used to evoke lost worlds of imagination, play and trustfulness, they are, through their very newness to the social world, seen as being closer to nature and so to our own true nature in some pre-social state. They are more like us than we are ourselves. And as with nature, there is nothing natural about this disposition. These visions of primal innocence or cruelty exist only in some conceptual Arcadia or Hobbesian nightmare. Noble savage: nasty brute; angels: devils; innate virtue and original sin. These are cultural constructs organised around the old lines of moral cleavage. But what is important is that these ideas of what we are truly like are a starting point for thinking about how we can live together. Each vision of the essential human has its own distinct implications for social form; its own different blueprint for social reproduction and continuity. So images of childhood not only take us back to a primal past; they take us forward to the end point of some social project. Just like real children in real families, they are the future. They bear the weight of all our individual and collective aspirations and all our fears about what cannot be known.

So the three images of childhood I want to talk about are not the simple moral prototypes of a primitive past, but these forward-looking versions of children in society: children who are what they are by virtue of their relationship to others. In terms of iconography they form a triptych of potent images in our dominant cultural discourses.

The centre-piece of this threefold vision is, appropriately enough, a mother and child with the intense interaction of a Madonna and Christ child, but nothing of their fragile piety. They are the mother/child dyad of post-war 'pro-natalism' as portrayed in Denise Riley's *War in the Nursery*. They are bonded by superglue and entwined in a million invisible attachments — the popularised product of a psychoanalytic imagination crossed with animal behaviourism.

The child is neither born all good nor all bad, though with more than a touch of infantile sexuality. She is essentially the achievement of welfarism; if good, she is the outcome of the right psycho/social circumstances. If deviant, the result of poor adjustment and in need of rehabilitation and reform. The mother too is a child; she is nurtured by the state.

The particular mother/child image I have in mind is one from my personal store of memories. Far from being a large gilded painting, it reflects the culture of post-war utility. It is the cover picture of my mother's cookery book. On it is another mother. She is a middle-class woman, kindly and smiling, a Mrs Do-as-you-would-be-done-by. Her arms encircle a happy, alert and healthy looking girl-child, who is learning to cook. These two, mother and daughter, are in matching aprons. Their heads are close enough to show that they, at least, have no problems with infestation. They are also looking at a cookery book. And, of course, it is the selfsame book as the one on which they appear. Their image goes on into infinity. Looking at this book with my mother, I am implicated in this relentless reproduction. I peer into a future of cheerful, protective mothers, their confidence based on working husbands and free professional state services, and of well-reared and contented children, eager to learn and responsive to the benign guidance of adults. And now, nearly half a century later, I am a little nostalgic for this vision of the world.

Granted, this dewy-eyed paternalism had its dark side — not least this culinary version of woman's destiny. Britain's basic social hierarchy was comparatively unchallenged by the new welfare state and the power structures of the traditional patriarchal family were reinforced by the paternalist ideal. A barrage of propaganda steered women from the workplace into the home; legislation kept children longer in school; the needs of a particular form of capitalism were served.

It is significant that the contemporary images of childhood, apart from the resourceful boys and girls who peopled the imagination of Enid Blyton *et al*, were dominantly those of child-in-family. Children were not individuals, but rather the result of collective effort. It was not part of the paternalist ideal to define them as having rights of their own, though they certainly had needs. The model does not recognise any opposition in the interests of the nations' citizens. State power, male power is the expression of the highest collective aspirations to co-operate and support each other in misfortune. It is not seen as oppressive or constraining of the individual, but rather nurturing and benign. Big Daddy knows best.

Of course, it had to go. Feminism and the fall of the full employment consensus saw to that. But what was so attractive — and so remarkable from the perspective of the fragmented nineties — was the optimism about human nature and collective confidence in the future, predicated as these were on high levels of trust in the reliability of those who knew what was good for us — state, parents and professionals. So these rather stolid, sexless looking children, who appeared in books and advertisements for the stream of new consumer durables hitting the market, were the heroes and heroines of an expansive narrative: a tale of

*Post-War Britain: nostalgia for a safer world of cheerful protective mothers and 'well reared, contented children' Credit: Hulton Getty*

national renewal and progress towards a safer, happier and more equitable world.

If this centre panel of our triptych makes the rearing of children look like a manageable project, not so the two images on the side panels. Indeed these children, child villain and child victim, are the centre of what has been frequently and superfluously called 'a moral panic' about the failure of the modern family to undertake this task. But the panic seems to go much deeper. It is about the underpinnings of the whole social enterprise, or, as the sociologists would have it, the collapse and failure of the modernist project. The collective optimism of paternalism and the Keynesian consensus has been replaced by a profound and lonely fear about the future; a change in economic framework has paralleled major changes in what anthropologists like Mary Douglas, author of *Risk and Blame*, think of as our cultural type — from the interdependent, taken-for-granted relations of hierarchy, to a type more fitting to a global market; a more individualistic, claims-based ideal, where power is contested by individuals and small groups. It is their rights, thinks Douglas, that we wish to protect, rather than social institutions which make for cohesion and provide a basis for the legitimation of expertise and authority. Now no-one knows best. If we have moved from the politics of Big Daddy, and the politics of Big Brother ended when the Wall came down, we are now into the politics of Little Brother, where the rules of the playground apply.

So these little faces spell danger. The word 'risk' is on everyone's lips. As Anthony Giddens says in *The Consequences of Modernity*, we have 'colonised the future' as an area of human concern. And this is not just concern over the savageries of nature, which in the old days would have been met with displays of social solidarity; nor is it just about the risks inherent in our technological attempts to control and harness it; nor our lack of trust in the goodwill of government or big corporations in risk management (though this is an area of frequent outraged appeal to the images of children, from children eating burgers in a school canteen, to the fuzzier, foetal images of 'children yet unborn' and 'generations to come'). There is a deeper fear of the potential for destruction by the brute within society and, worst of all, the beast within ourselves. It is this that our side panels represent. Children who are victims not just of state, corporate or even parental power, but of each other.

Child victim and child villain: they look at first like cherub and imp, the opposing prototypes of good and evil. Though they both have ordinary, sweet childish faces, the newsprint context does it all, putting a halo on one and devil horns on the other. Removing these impositions of the moral fundamentalism of the press, we can see that they too are just products of their time — kids from the playground. They are both capable of good and evil.

These children are not opposites, but two sides of the same coin. They are both part of a legalistic discourse about individual moral responsibility, rights and their infringement — a language that is now a dominant form for the framing of human relationships because it defines a space where libertarian right and libertarian left achieve uneasy congruence. The juxtaposition of their images in the media, Jamie Bulger and his killers, emphasises how one could not exist without the other. The child victim has not the essential, strong, untouchable innocence of the child of the romantic imagination. His innocence is defined only by his violation. He is the essence of human vulnerability, not goodness. Likewise, the child villains, despite their demonising by the press, are not essentially evil. In the Bulger case our barbarous legal system underlines this. Bulger's killers were tried in court. They were treated, at 10 years of age, as legal subjects, rational and autonomous and therefore capable of moral decisions. In other words, it was assumed that they could have chosen to do otherwise than they did. They are both vulnerable and capable of harm.

The villains are pictured alone, school photos, each child captured in a moment of isolation, staring into the camera. They are not children-in-family, the products of their psycho-social circumstances. The welfarist story has been conspicuous by its absence from accounts of our villains. For instance, evidence of welfare science experts in the Bulger case were given short shrift in court. Of course there was interest in the life story of the two boys. But this produced a destruction of the moral character of the parents rather than an understanding of the children. The guilt of their parents only served to underline their own guilt. It is significant that commentators looking for an explanation linger on the tantalising hint of sexual abuse in this story, of Jamie by his killers and of them by some other family member. It is as if, were this to be true, no further explanation or mitigation would be necessary. Being a victim is an explanation for villainy which the rights discourse can accommodate. Two sides of the same coin.

Bulger and his killers. What we see in their juxtaposition is the tension that lies at the heart of the liberal rule of law as a principle for social organisation. We are all potentially victims and villains; without internal or external controls we are all dangerous. These children represent a failure of family supervision and control, or self-control. They are pictured alone; they have left their families and entered the monitoring and controlling remit of the state. And this emphasises another dualism: that the state in the role of protector of citizens' rights is also potentially an invader of their freedoms; that state power as well as individual power can be abusive. And as relations in families mirror these wider concerns, male power, parental power, which in the discourse of paternalism is used on *behalf* of women and children, is also suspect. We are told by some child protection experts that children can only protect themselves from adult power by according adults less authority. This is a far cry from the community of interest of state, parent and child in our paternalist panel, where the idea of benevolent supportive authority eliminates this tension between protection and control. It was not, from a civil liberties point of view, that control was not there: it was subtler, more seductive and more penetrative in this gentler more pro-active form of family and state governance, operating in the name of the welfare of its citizens. Now the state has pulled out of welfare. In the playground there are no nice teachers to talk to us and supervise. (They are not paid enough.) Police vans cruise the perimeter road, ready to intervene if things get nasty.

It is not surprising, then, if we are fearful; nor that the video still of Jamie Bulger and his two killers as they leave the shopping centre hand in hand is, of all the images of children in the media, the one that has grabbed us most. This is a happy family snap. A small child reaches up to hold the hands of his two big brothers on either side. There is perfect trust. Trust from the child and trust from the viewer, because they have seen this scene a million times before. But now we know different. The message is that you can trust no-one, take nothing for granted: not the government, not your boss, not your doctor, your teacher or your social worker, not your neighbours, not the people on the street; not even your own parents and siblings and least of all yourself.

If we have colonised the future as an area of concern, we are also colonising the old terrain of the personal, high-trust relationships with our doubts — the personal has become the political. We go out into the world heavily armed with insurance, a lawyer on our shoulder, a contract in hand and an assertiveness manual in our back pocket. The discourse of empowerment provides a new therapeutic language for victims, a legalistic pathway to healing. It is as if a whole mighty edifice of institutionalised inequality will come tumbling down in the face of clearly made claims and confident negotiation. And perhaps it will. The only trouble is that for every new right, there is a new vulnerability. The more territory that we stake out in the name of rights and needs, the more we risk its invasion by others. It is the insight of economics, that dismal science, that if land is scarce, its price goes up.

So these children, victim and villain, are for us the symbol of an uncertain future. If they also stand for a crisis in the family, it is not the one that the purveyors of 'family values' identify, as they try to shore up

● ● ● ● ● ● ● ● ● ● ● ● ● ● ● ● ● ● ● ● ● ● ● ● ● ● ● ● ● ● ● ● ● ● ● ●

**For every new right there is a new vulnerability. The more territory we stake out in the name of rights and needs, the more we risk its invasion by others**

● ● ● ● ● ● ● ● ● ● ● ● ● ● ● ● ● ● ● ● ● ● ● ● ● ● ● ● ● ● ● ● ● ● ● ●

the old patriarchal family as a place of hierarchy and privacy, 'a bastion between the individual and the state'. This bastion fell some time ago. The altered power relations between the sexes; demographic changes; and have dismantled it brick by brick. But the biggest breach has been made by children. It was not the Children Act of 1989 that did this. Though it confirmed their legal status as individuals first and members of their family second, it addressed only their rights in relation to the state and not to their own family. It was the dramatic disclosure by children of sexual abuse in more and more families that meant a new alliance, a confessional relationship, between children and the state. This has exposed to public gaze the most intimate secrets of family life: what can be done in the name of love. The family will never be the same again.

So the 'crisis' is about a pressing need to negotiate a different way of living together and to find a new way of viewing the family. This would *not* be family as a moral individual, the dependent child of the paternalistic state finally induced by a stringent social-policy-as-behavioural-programme to leave home and stand on its own two feet. *Not* family as responsible provider of a commodity called 'care' to its members over the life cycle. *Not, horribile dictu*, family opened up further to the quasi market, 'the mixed economy of care' with children reconstructed as 'consumers of parental services' and parents as their 'care co-ordinators', made accountable by a complaints procedure and a 'Family Audit and Inspection Unit'. But, nevertheless, a family opened up to collective support wherever that is located, a site of flexible and variable relationships, and still separate enough to be a space where all its members can feel safe and cared for.

'The family' has always reconciled the unreconcilable, been a fine exponent of the art of 'both and'. The paternalist metaphor reconciled the tension between care, autonomy and control with the idea of benign authority. Now we are searching for a new guiding principle in line with a more libertarian ideal. But endless negotiation is exhausting. Not only are new rules of living yet to be hammered out, we do not even know the rules of the debate. Who contributes? Who has a voice? The state? The community? Professionals? Men? Women? Parents? Children? If men have retained their voice and women are gaining theirs, children of the family are very seldom heard. Perhaps it is time for us to take our icons off the wall and have a dialogue with real children. Perhaps the nub of our problem is that this is very hard for us to do. No-one who has listened to children from troubled families will doubt their vigilance on behalf of their parents, nor their clear-eyed perception of adult needs. If adults look after them because they are born helpless into this world, then children agree to be looked after and do not often call our bluff. But for adults to call *their* bluff would be the last act of paternalism; the recognition that there is no 'other': that we are all the same. And it is in the dropping of our hierarchies of difference that all our anxieties begin. ❏

*Marian Allsopp is a researcher and teacher in the area of child care*

# LOOKING AT
# KIDS

**INDEX: keeping an eye out on children around the world**

Kids are constantly making the news in Index. In Index 1/1995, Caroline Moorehead
tells the startling truth about 10-year-old soldiers in Africa. Ten years after the Chernobyl
disaster, children from the region express their ongoing fears, confusion and grief (Index
1/1996). Amy Adler explores the unprecedented peak of anxiety in America about
portraying child sexuality in art (Index 3/1996).

Each back issue of Index sells for £8 (or $10 in the US).
Outside of the UK or the US, please add £1/$2 postage per issue.

Enter my order for ❑ Index 1/1995   ❑ Index 1/1996   ❑ Index 3/1996

.................................................
Name

£/$........ enclosed  for........ back issues

.................................................
Address

❑ Cheque (UK£ or US$)   ❑ Visa/MC/AmEx

.................................................

.................................................
Card no.

.................................................

.................................................                    .................................................
               Postcode                                            Expires

33 Islington High St, London N1 9LH   Tel: 44 171 278 2313   **INDEX**

# Children in statistics

One quarter of the world's children live in south Asia

40 million children live on the streets of the world's cities; in 1988, 8,000,000 of them were on the streets of Sao Paolo, Brazil (population 32,000,000)

The average age of the homeless in the USA is 9

12 million children a year die before reaching 5, mostly from preventable diseases

Three US children die every day as a result of abuse or neglect

A child born in New York today is less likely to live to 5 than a child born in Shanghai

30% of children in developing countries do not complete 4 years of schooling

Children in the US are owed US$34 billion in unpaid child support

20% of all America's children live below the poverty line; 43.8% of America's black children live below the poverty line

In 1979, 1 in 10 children in the UK lived below the poverty line; in 1996, it was 1 in 3

2,000,000 children visit EuroDisney every year

A gun takes the life of a child every 2 hours in the USA; 50,000 children were killed by firearms between 1979 and 1991 — same as US casualties in the Vietnam War

Child mortality rates have fallen by 50% since 1946

In Liberia, children made up a quarter of all civil war combatants

In Angola, 7% of children had fired at somebody in 1995

In Sarajevo, 1 in 4 children have been wounded

In Rwanda, 114,000 children had been separated from their families by the end of 1994

In the UK, children begin to worry about being too fat by the age of 8

An extra US$30-40 billion would eradicate poverty by the year 2000

In California youths serve sentences 60% longer than adults for the same crimes

A baby born to an unskilled manual worker in the UK was twice as likely to die in its first year as a baby from a professional/managerial home

2,800 children were murdered in Columbia in 1991

85% of US child prostitutes have previously suffered rape, incest or abuse

1,000,000 children work in the Asian sex trade

1,000,000 children worldwide have been born HIV positive:

Children are the victims of summary execution in 32 countries

Children are tortured by the authorities in 11 countries

There are 100,000,000-200,000,000 child labourers worldwide

64,000 US children aged 14-17 were treated in hospital for work-related injuries in 1992

US child star of Home Alone, Macaulay Culkin is worth US$20 million

By age 15, between 20-25 per cent of British children have tried solvents or other drugs

3,568 legal abortions were performed on under 16-year-olds in the UK in 1988,

By the age of 18, young people have watched over 23,000 hours of television, many more than they have spent in the classroom

6,042 children are arrested every day in the USA

48 Brazilian orphans are available for adoption via the Internet

50% of Cambodians are under 15

70% of Indonesia's under 5s are malnourished according to a local health official

Ireland has the world's lowest infant mortality rate

4,000 children in the USA will be murdered by their parents this year

1.3 million US children run away from violence or rape every year

40% of murdered children were in the legal custody of social services at the time

2,000,000 girls between 4 and 12 undergo genital mutilation every year

At least 1,000,000 children a year are left motherless by death in childbirth

12% of 15-year-olds in the industrialised world smoke cigarettes every day

*Sources include:* The State of the World's Children *(1996);* Save the Children Review 1995-6; *The Progress of Nations 1996 (UNICEF website); Sandy Ruskin* Children in Europe; *Child Welfare League of America HN3898 @handsnet.org;* New Internationalist; *National Child Rights Alliance (website); The Internet Index (treese@OpenMarket.com); Children's Defense Fund (USA); Plant & Plant Risk Takers;* Free Labour World *(USA);* Freedom Review *(USA)*

*Compiled by Jesse Banfield and Nevine Mabro*

# MARIA MARGARONIS

# Talking about *Kids*

**The controversial film *Kids* was made at a time of unprecedented panic about children and sexuality and provoked calls for censorship. Yet this flawed melodrama is preferable to the adult silence that maims and destroys adolescent lives**

For many adults, adolescence is another country, fraught with half-remembered dangers. Its uncertain ground gives free rein to our anxieties about boundaries — between child and adult, innocence and ignorance, desire and exploitation. Meanwhile, teenagers' protean subcultures make their own sense out of the adult world, parental and commercial. Adolescents, more than most people, live by stories, trying out different ones to find out who they are and what they might become. But stories about teenagers — especially teenage sexuality — tend to be contested and heavily policed.

On the one hand, there's the urge to protect children from images meant to arouse feelings they can't yet assimilate, and from adults' exploitation of their immaturity. On the other, there's the temptation to solve a problem by suppressing it: the dangerous fantasy that childhood can be prolonged by keeping adolescents in the dark, like bulbs prepared for forcing. Both impulses are complicated by our envy of youth and its licence to act out, and by our guilt at the mess of many kids' lives: our failure to offer them a future worth growing up into, our uselessness in the face of AIDS and the enormous edifice of drug capitalism.

All these factors were at work in the media fuss about Larry Clark's *Kids*, released last year in the US (unclassified) and Britain (18 slightly cut), the latest in a long line of teen movies dating back to *Blackboard Jungle* to provoke calls for censorship. The arguments turned on the usual false dichotomy: would the film encourage teenagers to copy the behaviour it shows, or provide a valuable warning and focus for conversation? (Valerie Howarth, chief executive of the British charity Childline, went so far as to say, 'This film will not alert parents to the problems faced by teenagers because good parents will simply not want to watch it.') Its opponents saw the film as an exaggerated vision of hell verging on child pornography; its supporters, as a raw and honest portrait of one stream of adolescent life in New York City.

As usual, the truth lies somewhere in between. *Kids* records 24 hours in the lives of a loose group of friends, who roam the city free of adult supervision. Sixteen-year-old Jenny learns that she's caught the HIV virus from her first sexual contact with Telly, a boy who gets his kicks deflowering little girls. As she staggers through the darkening streets looking for him, he's busy sweet-talking his next victim into bed at a drunken, druggy party. Jenny arrives too late and passes out on the floor, where she is clumsily raped by Telly's envious sidekick: 'Don't worry Jenny it's me, Caspar, don't worry Jenny...'

The film gets its force from an unusual blend of loose, documentary style and melodramatic plotting. Watching feels like eavesdropping. The lens is perched at odd angles, almost like a security camera; the soundtrack hums with a messy mix of music and ambient New York noise. The kids themselves seem so real — their clothes, their speech, their loping, shambling gait, their shifty looks and subtle jockeying for position — that they almost obscure the hand of the director, pulling the strings of an old-fashioned cautionary tale.

The critics' more extreme anxieties don't hold water. No-one could possibly miss the movie's moral, or want to emulate its subjects' aimless lives. The sex scenes are too bleak to be exciting in any but the coldest, most mechanical way. But nor is *Kids* a masterpiece of radical realism. For all his vaunted fascination with teenagers, Clark dumbs down the complexities of their lives in a melodramatic update of an old tale, the virgin seduced and abandoned. The characters are very broadly drawn: the boys are uniformly selfish, the girls defined solely in terms of their sexuality. If they care about each other at all, they can't express it. When Jenny learns that she has HIV, her friend Ruby can only trot out upbeat clichés: 'You'll work it out, it's going to be okay...' Because the kids are allowed no subjectivity they tend to seem alien, cartoonish beyond reach. In that sense the film is exploitative, meant to shock (as adolescents sometimes like to) rather than to engage.

And yet, *Kids* also shows up huge inadequacies in the way we usually talk or are allowed to talk about adolescents. The events it shows do happen. A quarter of new HIV infections in the US occur in people under 20; in a recent US survey, seven out of 10 girls who had sex before age 14, and six out of 10 who had sex before age 15, said they had it involuntarily. (On the other hand, most US adolescents don't have intercourse until their mid to late teens, and condom use at first penetration has doubled since the 1980s, though only to 48 per cent.) But we rarely hear those kids' own voices or see how they experience their lives; rarely get to know what they're about, not as a problem to be solved but just as themselves.

The most interesting parts of *Kids* happen on the sidelines, beyond the plot's judgemental grip. They have to do with hanging out, with the texture of teenagers' lives in the city — the long rattling subway rides, the half-furnished apartments, the swoop of skateboards in Washington Square. In this adult-free zone, class and racial lines are less important than a pecking order based on tiny nuances of coolness and bravado. One sequence cuts between a group of girls and a group of boys, talking about sex with giggly energy that feels live and improvised. Boy talk: 'Girls love to suck dick — that's why girls live longer than guys, that sperm is full of vitamin C or some shit, man.' Girl talk: 'I *hate* sucking dick.' 'Have you ever swallowed it before, though?' 'Those little sperms, they, like, get stuck in your teeth...' (Shrieks of laughter.) The gender gap is obvious, funny and painful. The boys dwell on the strategies of conquest; the girls talk about what pleases them, the difference between fucking, having sex and making love. Though the girls' forthrightness sometimes seems atypical there is liberating, vital information in the way they put things, the way they compete and relate to each other and egg each other on.

In her recent book *Going All the Way: Teenage Girls' Tales of Sex, Romance and Pregnancy* — a very different product of an adult's fascination with adolescent lives — Sharon Thompson reported that many girls she spoke to said that nothing they had read or seen told them 'how they would feel, what they would want, what would worry them, what the odds for or against their dreams coming true were'. It would be naive to think that greater openness can fix so many prematurely broken lives. But unless teenagers can hear the stories they live by in their own voices and recognise them as stories, they can't begin to change the script. Unless adults listen too — not to judge or advise, but just to hear — they have no hope of helping. Anyone who doubts that silence can be lethal might

*Casper from Kids, USA 1996: 'hanging out in the adult free zone' Credit: Electric Pictures*

consider the recent killing of a newborn baby by its upper-middle-class teenage parents in a Delaware motel room. What combination of shame, guilt, isolation, denial, ignorance, *folie à deux* and fear of disappointing their families made those kids do nothing and tell no-one about a pregnancy so violently unwanted that it ended in murder?

*Kids* was made in a time of unprecedented panic about children and sexuality. In the last few years, fears of child abuse have led to witch-hunts in day care centres on both sides of the Atlantic. Paedophiles have replaced terrorists as public bogeymen; the legislation known in the US as Megan's Law, which points out convicted sex offenders to their neighbours after their release, now has its advocates in Britain too. Photographs of naked children are suspect, whether they are made by artist Sally Mann or by the British parents reported to the police by Boots the Chemists for taking snapshots of their seven-year-old daughter in the bath. Not long ago a Massachusetts three-year-old was taken into care because her mother admitted to having sexual feelings while breast feeding. In his new book, *As If*, about the murder of two-year-old James Bulger by two older boys, Blake Morrison wonders, 'Who's to say what's innocent anymore where a small child is involved? What's abuse and what is not?' He does not go on to ask, what has made it so hard for us to tell?

That may be the question we have to answer in order to make the careful distinctions necessary to protect children from real abuse and adolescents from the damage done by ignorance and isolation. In the meantime, when sexual expression is under threat, when 'abstinence only' sex education is enshrined in America's new welfare law, when adolescent lives are at risk, even a flawed, melodramatic film like *Kids* is better than decorous silence. ❏

*Maria Margaronis worked for 10 years as a journalist in New York with the* Nation *and the* Village Voice. *She now lives in London*

# EDWARD LUCIE-SMITH

# Eros and innocence

**Images of childhood in western art reflect society's changing attitudes to children. While the erotic force of past masters is beyond reproach or banishment, the intrusion of the camera provokes outrage and censoriousness**

WHILE showing an ever-increasing tolerance for other forms of sexual representation, contemporary culture shows a tremendous sensitivity to depictions of nudity where children or even adolescents under the current age of consent are involved. The only other images which now fall into the same category of the strictly forbidden are bestiality and scatology. Even these do not seem to arouse the same feelings of rage and horror in otherwise libertarian spectators. The famous Pompeiian group of a satyr coupling with a goat has been reproduced without apology in a number of recent publications on Roman erotic art, or on erotic art in general. So has Rembrandt's etching of a woman pissing.

There are, of course, very good reasons for this disgust, and also perhaps some bad ones. Much that we see on television, or reported in the press, reminds us that ours is a society obsessed not only with manifestations of sexuality in children, but with our own sexual feelings towards them. Two recent examples will suffice. One is the recent murder of six-year-old JonBenét Ramsey of Boulder, Colorado, a prominent competitor on the child beauty pageant circuit which flourishes in the USA, and the public reaction to this event. The stories about JonBenét were illustrated with photographs of children dressed and made up to resemble sexually mature adults, and radiating in consequence an inappropriate allure. The other is the ever-increasing publicity given in the media to the phenomenon of 'sex tourism'. A recent article in *The Times* detailed how 'hundreds of thousands of western men flock to the east each year to have sex with children,' and told a heartbreaking tale of exploitation:

'The girls look happy,' said the bearded customer peering through the glass. 'I'll take number 28.' That was Concordia and over the next few hours the young Filipino prostitute was brutally raped. Later she needed surgery on her vagina and her anus...

Perhaps the only surprising thing here is the reluctance felt by some people to acknowledge a link between the child beauty pageant phenomenon and the darker happenings detailed in *The Times*' report on sexual mores in the Philippines, Thailand and Sri Lanka.

Things are not, however, as simple as they seem at first, either practically or morally. Sexual obsession with children is something which increasingly preoccupies policemen, psychologists, and fringe practitioners of various sorts. Britain has recently seen a series of investigations into paedophilia in officially-run children's homes — first in Northern Ireland, and now in Wales. Some of the allegations seem all too well founded. In the USA, and to a lesser degree in Britain, there have been instances of families split apart by so-called Recovered Memory syndrome, where an adult, after a period of severe depression and perhaps of psychiatric counselling, suddenly 'recalls' instances of sexual abuse by parents. In some other cases, allegations of sexual abuse have been made by children, encouraged by social workers, which have turned out to be almost certainly false. I say 'almost certainly' because accusations of this kind are notoriously difficult to disprove. The resemblance to seventeenth-century witch-hunts, where the original accusation of practising witchcraft was often made by young girls, has nevertheless often been striking.

It is into this context, to phrase it bluntly one of near-hysteria, that the debate about sexualised representations of children has to be put. I say 'sexualised' rather than simply 'nude' because one of the things which seems to have happened in contemporary culture is that we have lost the ability to divorce nudity from sex. Western art inherited from antiquity the image of the naked child, first as a personification of Eros, and secondly (there is a slight contradiction here) as a personification of innocence. There are numerous paintings and large decorative schemes, dating from the fifteenth to the eighteenth centuries, in which these nude children play a prominent part. It is only occasionally that we are aware of a sexual frisson. Two well-known bronzes by Donatello, the *David* and the *Attis*, are cases in point. We know from literary sources that Donatello was homosexual, and both these sculptures seem to speak of a personal attraction to pubescent boys, as do two celebrated later works — Parmigianino's *Eros Carving His Bow in Vienna*, and Caravaggio's *Amore Vincitore* in Berlin. The effect of these masterpieces is so complex, both culturally and emotionally, and they are so integral to the story of western art, that no-one has yet proposed they be banished from sight.

In the eighteenth century, especially in France, there was a change of emphasis. It became fashionable to show children, frequently naked, engaged in versions of adult occupations and pursuits. Often the children are shown kissing or embracing. There are two strands here — one harmless, one less so. An aspect of the Rococo was its jesting trivialisation both of the solemnities of mythology and the drudgery of the everyday world. Rococo pictures of naked children suggest that everything, myth and fact, can be homogenised as the materials for a harmless frolic. Nothing, these pictures and sculptures tell us, is to be taken too seriously. But Rococo artists, Boucher and Fragonard in particular, also idealised girls in early adolescence as sexual objects. Boucher's famous *Miss O'Murphy*, bottom up on her sofa, was reputedly a mistress of Louis XV, and one of the inhabitants of the libertine king's harem at the Parc aux Cerfs.

THE Rococo period in France lies on the cusp of a profound change in attitudes towards childhood in general. This was largely brought about by the writings of Jean-Jacques Rousseau (who abandoned his own children in orphanages where, given the condition of such institutions at the time, they died more likely than not without reaching maturity). Essentially what Rousseau did was to take the Christian idea of Original Sin and turn it on its head. In his idealised universe, children became the vessels of everything that was pure and true, and that was later corrupted by experience of the world. Where the erotic imagination of many of his contemporaries was concerned, this brought the not yet sexually mature into focus in an entirely new and not at all healthy way. One can see this kind of sexual imagining at work in many of the paintings of Jean-Baptiste Greuze, the artist whom Rousseau's fellow-philosopher, Denis Diderot, raised up as a morally superior alternative to Boucher. Greuze's

*Caravaggio 'Love Victorious': beauty and seduction Credit: Visual Arts Library/London*

characteristic canvases of young girls cradling some symbolic object —
weeping over a broken jug, for instance — combine prurience with overt
erotic content in about equal measure.

Greuze, in turn, set a pattern for many nineteenth-century depictions
of children. In Britain, Victorian society sentimentalised children —
Dickens's treatment of the character of Little Nell in *The Old Curiosity
Shop* is a notorious example — but at the same time exploited them. The
child prostitution we currently deplore in Thailand and the Philippines
was at that time rampant in London itself.

The nineteenth century also saw a very significant technological
development, the birth of photography, which, almost from its
beginnings, was used for erotic purposes. The most famous Victorian
photographer of little girls was, of course, Lewis Carroll, who sometimes
recorded his subjects fairly skimpily clothed, but never in openly erotic
poses. This famous series of images is, nevertheless, it is generally agreed,
the record of an obsession which was basically sexual in origin.

The aesthetics of photography have been much debated in recent
decades, with notable contributions from the French philosopher Roland
Barthes and the American writer Susan Sontag. In a significant passage in
her book *On Photography*, published in 1977, Sontag avers that: 'A
photograph is not just an encounter between an event and a
photographer, picture-taking is an event in itself, and one with ever more
peremptory rights — to interfere with, to invade, or to ignore whatever
is going on.' At another point in the same book she notes: 'All that
photography's program of realism actually implies is the belief that reality
is hidden. And being hidden it is something to be unveiled.' If we put
these two statements against the general historical background I have
outlined above, we begin to see, I think, why certain images of children
— children seen in situations which can be construed as erotic — now
seem peculiarly threatening and arouse, on occasion, almost
uncontrollable feelings of outrage. These feelings have on occasion been
excited by images made, it seems, completely innocently — for example,
by nude snapshots made by parents of their own children, sent for
development to a high street chemist.

If the debate about child pornography centres on photographs (and on
the related media of video and film) this is for a number of obvious
reasons. One is that these are the commonest, the most widely available
means of image-making. Images, by common consensus, are a more

potent means of arousing erotic feeling than the written word. Another is that the photograph is privileged because (unlike a drawing or a painting) it implies the presence of a live subject. It is not simply the embodiment of something imagined but not necessarily seen. Now that Rousseau has collided with Freud photographic images of children which are made with sexual intent, or which, though not so made, nevertheless excite sexual feeling in some spectators, seem peculiarly threatening. Though we know children do have sexual impulses, we prefer not to be brutally confronted with evidence of these. Still less do we like to be confronted with images which may, at some deep level, arouse unacceptable feelings in ourselves. We cannot, despite our familiarity with Freudian concepts, deal with the idea that parental love or its surrogates may contain a barely controlled sexual element.

Our extreme self-consciousness about images of this kind has had a curious result. During a decade when the boundaries of tolerance, certainly in the English-speaking world, have gradually loosened to the point where almost any sexual image can be published or exhibited, they have become noticeably tighter where photographic representations of children are involved. It is not Robert Mapplethorpe's photographs of male S&M activities that now cause concern, but his picture of a little girl throwing up her skirt to reveal her pudenda: the record of a spontaneous moment of exhibitionism of a sort very common in small children. Even Edward Weston's beautiful frontal torso of his young son has become the kind of image that publishers are reluctant to deal with. In these cases, the standard excuse is made: 'It is not, you understand, that I am disturbed by this particular image myself. It's just that other people might take it the wrong way.' ❏

*Edward Lucie-Smith* is a well-known UK writer and broadcaster on art. His most recent book is ArToday *(Phaidon 1996).* Movements in Art Since 1945: Issues and Concepts *was reissued in 1995 by Thames and Hudson in their* World of Art series

# The dark side of the beach

*Writing on the sand: a child prostitute names his price*

'Sex Tourism' from the West to the holiday resorts of Asia is widespread and well documented. Legislation designed to punish offenders from Europe and elsewhere is only now beginning to take effect. Meanwhile, Sri Lanka is the latest to join an expanding market pioneered by Bangkok and Manila. Our photographer secured his pictures by posing as a tout for would be clients en route for the beaches

**Photographs by Stephen Gill © Panos Pictures**

*Prostitute, pimp and brothel keeper*

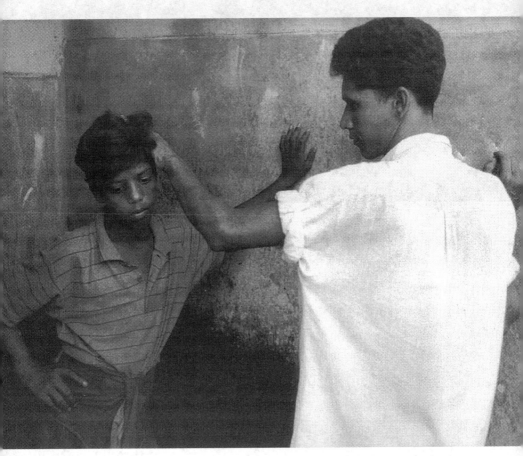

*Modelling for the client, pimp to hand*

*Fear, innocence, seduction*

*Sold for sex in Colombo*

# CAROLINE MOOREHEAD

# All the world's children

**It promised a better world but almost every ill the UN Convention on Children set out to remedy has grown worse**

O F THE hundreds of haunting stories heard by Graça Machel's team last year when they were preparing the United Nations report on the Impact of Armed Conflict on Children was one they could not forget. It was told by a nine-year-old Liberian girl. She was describing an attack on her village by one of the marauding armed gangs that have kept the country in a state of permanent civil war for the last seven years. She told how she had watched while '19 or 20' villagers were shot, 'mostly old people who couldn't walk fast'. She said that her uncle had been killed by a bullet to the head, and that she had looked on while her father was forced to mutilate his body. Later, she saw her nine-year-old cousin raped.

Concern over violence towards children, teaching children to be violent and the effects on children of being continually made to witness violence, rather than the fate of street children and physical abuse, has become the major preoccupation of the late-1990s in the human rights world. Statistics here have not lost their power to shock. Over the last decade, some two million children have been killed in wars, six million seriously injured or disabled, and almost 30 million turned into refugees. In Sarajevo, so it is said, more than half the children were shot at, and 66 per cent found themselves in situations in which they expected to die. In Angola, 67 per cent watched people being tortured, beaten and hurt, many of them members of their own families. In Rwanda, all but a few children lost relations, 16 per cent of them surviving by hiding underneath their dead bodies. It was after the Rwanda killings of the Tutsi that children interviewed said that they did not care whether or not they ever grew up.

The Convention on the Rights of the Child turns seven this year. Of all human rights conventions ever to be drafted it has been signed and ratified the fastest: all but a handful of countries — the USA having proved singularly dilatory — are already party to its articles, which are succinct and all embracing. They promise not just a better, but a good world for children, all the more satisfactory as 90 per cent of the world's two billion children live in countries that hastened to ratify.

As with the Convention on Torture, however, it is all something of a sham. The Convention on Children is being violated, systematically and contemptuously, and no countries violate it more energetically than those that were quickest to sign. Almost every ill it set out to remedy has grown worse in the years since it was drafted. At the same time, the world has never had more human rights organisations devoted to the interests of children, and never have the international agencies proved as concerned for their welfare. Reports pour out daily — on female circumcision, land-mines, prostitution. For the most part they have a sad and defeated ring to them.

IN 1945, Europe was awash with refugees, some 40 million people forced from their homes by war or driven over borders by the Nazis' deportation policies, and now struggling to go home. Many were desperately struggling to find people they had lost or been parted from, and there is no more heartbreaking memory of that war than the posters of photographs of lost children, or children seeking their parents, that were hung in every police station and railway terminus. Below the pictures of babies, barely able to sit up, were printed the words: 'Who am I?'

The same phenomenon is being repeated today in Rwanda, where 100,000 children have been separated from their parents, most of them aged between eight and two, the moment at which they cease to be carried by their mothers, yet too young to be able to explain who they are. Greatly helped by modern computers and databases, UNICEF and the International Committee of the Red Cross have done a remarkable job in reuniting some 33,000 of these children with surviving relations. As in post-war Europe, photographs of the children are posted throughout the refugee camps. In Rwanda, the children are known as 'unaccompanied', a word that has a somehow comforting ring, as if it were all a journey soon to end in a reunion. What these children have witnessed and endured is appalling to contemplate.

Africa has become the continent in which children learn about war. Uganda, Burundi, Zaire, Somalia, Angola, Mozambique, Liberia and Sudan have all lived through — and in many places continue to live through — a permanent state of civil war, in which children as young as seven have been recruited, kidnapped or coerced into joining armed

● ● ● ● ● ● ● ● ● ● ● ● ● ● ● ● ● ● ● ● ● ● ● ● ● ● ● ● ● ● ●

**The Convention on the Rights of the Child is being violated, systematically and contemptuously, and no countries violate it more energetically than those that were quickest to sign**

● ● ● ● ● ● ● ● ● ● ● ● ● ● ● ● ● ● ● ● ● ● ● ● ● ● ● ● ● ● ●

groups, be they government forces or guerrillas. The Convention stipulates 15 as the lowest age at which a child may be a soldier, and the campaigns to raise that to 18, begun during drafting, have intensified ever since. But as automatic weapons like AK-47s, so light and so easy to assemble that they pose no problems for robust small boys, spread out through the civilian population in the wake of ceasefires and peace settlements that seldom last very long, so ever smaller children are needed to build up fighting forces. A third of Liberia's soldiers are said to be children. They act as porters and guards, they carry messages and stand at checkpoints. Because they are quick and agile, they are sent into no man's land to bring back weapons. Biddable, frightened, dependent, they make excellent killers. Rites of passage into the brotherhood of soldiers are said to include the execution of prisoners and the eating of their hearts and livers to absorb courage. Drugs — amphetamines or a mixture of cane juice and gunpowder — are given to the children to 'make them strong and brave'.

In Sudan's long-running conflict between the Islamic military government and the opposition forces of the Sudan People's Liberation Army, the Nuba children of the hills of South Kordofan province are doubly at risk: from government forces, who round up boys for their militias in sweeps to 'cleanse the mountains', and from the SPLA, who separate children from their families to ensure a reservoir from which to draw recruits. In Khartoum not long ago, there were said to be 3,000 boy soldiers, aged between seven and 11. From the camps to which they are taken come stories of starvation and disease. One boy who escaped, part of a group of 129 young Sudanese trying to reach the safety of the Kenyan border, told an aid worker not long ago: 'When we crossed the river, the crocodiles got 34 of us.' Sudan, like Liberia, is a country where there are few children today who know the meaning of peace. Twelve years of war have produced children who have never learnt to read or write, who spend their days practising with weapons, and who grow larger, stronger and more brutalised every day.

Not all these children, and in some places not many of them, survive. The technology that brought light, cheap weapons to civilians has also brought small, cheap land-mines, all the deadlier for being invisible in grass and for continuing to explode for decades if touched. Recent campaigns led by the International Committee of the Red Cross and supported by an unusually united front of lobbyists all over the world have failed to bring about a total ban on the production and sale of land-mines, of which the UN says that 110 million now lie unexploded in the fields and countryside of the developing world. Too expensive and too time-consuming to remove, they maim and kill long after the fighting stops, their main victims being women and children, tending herds or gathering grass. The children who do survive are more likely to be severely injured: because a child's bones grow faster than the surrounding tissue, the wound can require repeated amputations. Few of the countries who have hastened to ratify the Convention on Children have seen the irony in refusing to be party to the one on Inhumane Weapons.

IF AFRICAN children are at the forefront in learning about war — rapidly being caught up by those in the Balkans and the former Soviet Union — Asian children know about work. It is easy to forget, in the plethora of reports published today about child labour, that right up until the early 1970s child slavery seemed to belong to a shadowy Victorian past. It was only when the Anti-Slavery Society in London started to produce reports on children working in carpet factories in Morocco, small girls forced to sit at looms weaving tiny stitches all day long, that the reliance of much of the developing world on the work of children began to be noticed. The most recent of many UNICEF reports published last year puts the figure of child workers at around 250 million under the age of 14. They work in stone quarries and match factories, at looms and in the fields they

• • • • • • • • • • • • • • • • • • • • • • • • • • • • •

# Universal and binding

'**A** century that began with children having virtually no rights is ending with them having the most powerful legal instrument that not only recognises but protects their human rights.' Carol Bellamy, UNICEF executive director.

The uniqueness of the UN Convention on the Rights of the Child stems from the fact that it is the first legally binding international instrument to incorporate the full range of human rights, children's civil and political rights as well as their economic, social and cultural rights. It sets minimum legal and moral standards for the protection of children's rights that are binding on all states that are party to the convention; where such standards are not enforced by national law the higher standard always applies.

The convention stipulates these general principals: that each child enjoys full rights without discrimination or distinction; that the child's best interests shall always be the prime consideration in determining all actions affecting children; that every child has an inherent right to life and states must ensure child survival and development; that children have the right to be heard.

• • • • • • • • • • • • • • • • • • • • • • • • • • • • •

pick rags and crops, they carry heavy loads and wash cars. They earn very little. Many start work at the age of five and reach adulthood deformed, sick and illiterate, having spent their entire childhoods working in dusty, hot rooms in noise that permanently injures their ears. Exposure to biological and chemical agents is said to cause more deaths among children today than tetanus, polio and whooping cough. This is violence too.

India, with between 60 and 115 million child workers, is said to have more than any other country in the world. Fifteen million of them are 'bonded', child slaves working off debts incurred by families. While India has some of the most stringent laws on labour conditions, and accuses its critics of wishing to practise protectionist policies, there are few signs today of any real will to protect the children by enforcing them. Campaigners say that child labour is bedevilled by myths, all of which mitigate against improvements. These range from a comforting assumption that child labour only takes place in the developing world — there is no rich country without its child workers, most of whom are the children of immigrants, Gypsies or minority groups — to a suggestion that children work exclusively in export industries. (ILO calculates that the truth is nearer to five per cent). A sad lesson was learnt not long ago when, on the basis of a belief that the only way to curb child labour was to impose sanctions on employers of children, the Harkin Bill was introduced into the US Congress, prohibiting the import of products made by children under 15. So great was the threat felt by the Bangladesh garment industry, which exports 60 per cent of its products to the USA, that child workers, most of them girls, were immediately sacked. Later some of these girls were traced by researchers wishing to assess the impact of the Harkin Bill. Many were found in jobs far less safe than the garment industry, earning considerably less money; some had become prostitutes. In 1996, the ILO announced that it would draft a new Convention to target 'intolerable' forms of child labour.

Prostitution and the trafficking of young girls is, like child labour, a subject of myths. As with labour, they are designed to comfort and obfuscate; in the same way, they distort the truth. The first World Congress against the Sexual Exploitation of Children was held in Stockholm in the summer of 1996, as a reflection of anxiety at signs that it was spreading. Those who gathered learned that child pornography and prostitution are not confined, as many had assumed, to the developing countries, and that they were not only exploited by tourists, but were ingrained in the cultures of a number of southeast Asian countries, as part of the general discrimination against women. The existence of efficient and highly profitable international trafficking networks has been recognised, with children regularly bought and sold across borders. After considerable stalling, the British government has finally agreed to join 13 other countries in introducing the prosecution of British tourists, in the UK, who have sexually exploited children overseas.

FOR some years now, Amnesty International and Human Rights Watch have been describing the death squads at work in Brazilian cities. Said to have been set up in the mid-1950s by senior police officers to combat rising crime, over the year, the killers turned their attention to street children. Their numbers grew steeply as peasants left the Brazilian countryside to swell the population of the towns; they keep alive by begging, washing cars and picking through rubbish. In 1990, UNICEF calculated that there were 7.5 million children and adolescents living and

PAUL SMITH/PANOS PICTURES

*Guatemala City 1990s: Nelson (11) sleeps it off; Nancy, seven months pregnant, takes her turn
with the glue; Julio (16) expectant father waits*

● ● ● ● ● ● ● ● ● ● ● ● ● ● ● ● ● ● ● ● ● ● ● ● ● ● ● ● ● ● ● ● ● ● ● ●

# To be born a girl

Not long ago, a group of young girls recruited by the Tamil Tigers in Sri Lanka as child soldiers were interviewed by a foreign journalist. Dressed in crisp military uniforms, cleaning their shiny kalashnikovs, the girls were full of praise for their new lives. It was wonderful to escape the drudgery at home, they told the journalist, and it was even better to leave behind all the restrictions that Sri Lankan society imposes on women. What none of them knew was how profoundly they would soon be exploited: as child soldiers, made to do some of the more dangerous tasks, and as girls, forced to act first as servants, then as prostitutes for the men.

The kind of work children do, and the ways in which they are most abused, is usually broken down into seven main areas: forced and bonded labour, industrial and plantation work, street work, work for families, girls' work, domestic and sexual exploitation. Girls are involved in all of them — but almost exclusively so in the last three. While much of what girls do is hidden, and they are often treated as invisible, as if somehow they do not exist, it seems that the UN Convention is most persistently violated with regard to girls. Violations over the whole spectrum — from household chores carried out after full days of work, to death.

No figures are harder to come by than those covering sexual exploitation, but non-governmental organisations believe that there are at least one million girls who are lured or forced into the billion-dollar sex industry each year. Village loan sharks act as procurers for city brothels, lending money to families that their daughters have to pay off. The girls may end up trafficked long distances and across borders. Few ever come home. A recent Human Rights Watch report, *A Modern Form of Slavery*, looked at Burmese girls in Thailand's brothels. Some were only 10. All were mistreated, frightened and prey to diseases.

In China, home to one-fifth of the world's children, 65 million children live in poverty. Preference for boys is marked. Fearful of China's one-child policy, parents do not register their girls, waiting for a son. Here, as across India and Pakistan, selective abortion and infanticide of girls are common.

Nine out of 10 of the children working as domestics are girls. Haiti, one of the few places where a reliable survey has been carried out, has an estimated 250,000 child servants. Twenty per cent of them are aged between seven and 11.

Some two million girls, between four and 12, undergo genital mutilation every year. In Somalia, the number of girls mutilated is believed to be 98 per cent. *CM*

● ● ● ● ● ● ● ● ● ● ● ● ● ● ● ● ● ● ● ● ● ● ● ● ● ● ● ● ● ● ● ● ● ● ● ●

working on Brazil's streets.

As violence in these chaotic cities spread, and robberies rose, so the finger of blame for a country in economic and social collapse was pointed at the street children. The death squads, and the vigilantes who flourished alongside, turned to killing children. It proved easy to catch them. Dazed by sniffing glue or the residue left over from the production of cocaine, their reaction times were very slow. In 1993, according to the Brazilian paper *O Dia*, there were 68 death squads active in a single neighbourhood of Rio de Janeiro. That summer, complaints at the growing numbers of child deaths turned into public outrage after a gang of hooded men opened fire on 50 children sleeping outside the church of Candelaria. Eight of the children died, four instantly, one as he ran away, two others hunted down in nearby gardens. The eighth died of his wounds a few days later. For a while, the killings slowed down. Today, street children are again disappearing, their bodies turning up, sometimes mutilated, in rubbish dumps.

Not long before the massacre outside the Brazilian church, Colombia, the country with the infamous reputation of having more murders than any other country in the world, had experienced its own street-child massacre, and its own public outcry. It was in Colombia that the term *'limpieza social'* or 'social cleansing', ridding society of 'disposables', entered the vocabulary of human rights. During an epidemic of violent killings of children — which rose to 70 per cent in a single year, until six children were dying every day — an incident took place one day in a town called Villatina, in east Medellin.

At 9pm on the evening of 15 November 1992, eight children, one of them eight-year-old Johanna Mazo, the others members of a Christian group called 'Walking Builders of the Future', were standing together on a street corner when three cars drew up. Twelve plain-clothed people got out, one masked, all carrying guns. The boys, suspecting them to be police, prepared to get out their identity cards. The men fired. In the panic that followed, some of the boys tried to protect Johanna. Shortly before dying, one boy told his mother that he had recognised among the killers a member of police intelligence, F-2. It was assumed that the killings were in revenge for policemen killed earlier in skirmishes with local gangs.

Unusually, the inhabitants of Villatina protested. Parents of the dead boys pushed for an inquiry. The whole district went on to alert when death threats were made against them and unmarked cars took to patrolling the streets. Just the same, senior police officers decided that there would be an investigation, and a number of policemen were arrested.

In the weeks that followed, the arrested men were transferred; the investigation itself was moved to the capital to protect the lives of the investigators. And there the matter stalled. Witnesses were threatened and fell silent. For a time, while it looked as if some kind of justice would follow, a mood of near optimism came to Villatina: new schools were started and dialogue opened with the street gangs. But Brigadier Hernandez, the man said to have ordered the killing of the children, was not moved from his post at the head of F-2. Little by little, less was said about a trial. The killing of the 'disposables' began again. Meanwhile, the murder and violent bullying of street children seems to be spreading. No longer confined to South America, there are reports of children being taken by police off the streets of India's major cities, only to 'disappear' in custody; and children are said to be wounded and beaten up by police in Turkey (see p165), Bulgaria and Kenya.

S INCE the early 1970s, Survival International has been campaigning for the rights of tribal people. Over the years they have witnessed and reported every kind of repression, from displacement to murder, but never found the tribal people to respond by killing themselves. In 1993, the Innu in Canada, moved away from their lands and hunting grounds, began to commit suicide. Among them were children. In Brazil, the Kaiowa, watching the steady destruction of their lands, are also turning to suicide. Most of those who die are children. The youngest yet recorded is Lucienne Ortiz. She was nine.

It would not be fair to see all the developments of recent years as losses. More progress has been made in terms of child health and education in the last 50 years than in the previous 2,000. Largely due to programmes run by UNICEF, the number of children who die every year has been halved, while in just under 20 years, the number of children vaccinated has risen from five to 80 per cent. The world they grow up to see grows more violent all the time. ❑

*Caroline Moorehead is a writer and broadcaster specialising in human rights. She is currently writing a history of the International Committee of the Red Cross*

*Delhi, India: child labourers demand their rights Credit: Paul Smith/Panos Pictures*

## URVASHI BUTALIA

# So many Shivas

**Over 100 million children work as bonded labourers in India, a form of slavery from which there is no escape and to which they are doomed for life. The law is ineffectual and, despite the efforts of abolitionists, the subject remains ringed by a wall of silence**

SHIVA Murugan was eight years old when he was killed by his employer, Ganesh Rajput. Like many other children of the same age — and others who are both younger and older — Shiva worked at a roadside eating place in Wani, Maharashtra. He hadn't chosen his job, nor could he ever escape from it: he had been sold, in perpetuity, to his employer by his uncle. When he did try to escape, his employer beat and burned him to death. Shiva never had a chance.

THERE are something like 111 million Shivas in India, roughly 12 per cent of the population — child labourers sold, often by their own families, into a form of slavery that has come to be known as bonded labour. These children are tied to their employers for life, and belong to them body and soul. In some industries, such as the match factories in Sivakasi, even unborn children are pledged to the factory owners against maternity loans to the parents. They have no hope of escape. Those who try, more often than not, meet the same fate as Shiva.

The death of one child is a signal to others that they must not even attempt to escape, and so the circle of fear continues. A conspiracy of silence surrounds the subject: those who see and know what is happening choose not to speak; the children continue to be exploited and victimised. Sexual abuse is also widespread, but the taboo surrounding it is even more powerful.

Attempts to stop such exploitation of children have met with a variety of responses: 'without the income these children are able to bring in, they (or their families) would starve'; 'if child labour was actually banned by law, what is the guarantee that these children would get what every child has a right to — an education, a childhood, a life?' And so on.

And there are equally strong rebuttals. For every child who works, assert the opponents of child labour, there is an adult who can do the work. For every adult who condones child labour there is a child who will be denied the joys of childhood.

There is some truth in all of this. Poverty-stricken families are often forced to send children out to work; there is no guarantee that if children were not forced to work, they would actually have a childhood. In many parts of India, it is believed that the birth of a child simply means another pair of working hands.

Recently, in response to campaigns and demands by activist groups to stop the exploitation of children, the Indian government enacted a law: the Regulation and Abolition of Child Labour Act. Like many other pieces of right-thinking legislation, this Act also lacks teeth. 'How,' says Vasudha Daghamvar, a lawyer and activist, 'can you regulate something you want to abolish? The moment you speak of regulation, you're recognising something, giving it legal status.'

That apart, the law is full of loopholes. It bans children (defined in Indian law as 'any individual under 14 years of age') from working in hazardous processes, but not hazardous places. Thus, for example, a child may be in a glass-producing factory, or a fireworks factory, in the presence of noxious fumes, but may not be working directly on glass blowing or firework making. He/she may instead be serving tea, or sweeping and swabbing — and that is not banned. The list of 'industries' the law earmarks as hazardous is by no means exhaustive. It totals 14, and doesn't include things like agriculture, or food stalls. And, what is more, the law doesn't ban children working in a family, so children can make carpets, as long as they are under their parents' supervision. It's also well known that one of the most prevalent forms of children's bonded labour is work in tea and food stalls. 'The Act gives a very limited definition of the word,' say activists. 'For us, *anything* that prevents the child from getting an education, or having a childhood, is hazardous.'

Poverty-stricken parents often say: 'why should we keep children with us? If they work, at least they will have something to eat.' But there is another reality: employers, who are more often than not exploitative, prefer children because they are more pliable, willing to work for less money, and, of course, they do not form unions.

'It's not as if employers don't recognise this,' says Daghamvar, 'that is why they are so keen to get hold of children.' One of the things employers very consciously do, point out activists, is actively prevent children from developing any skills. As a result, they are unable to go out and find other work. As children they're tied to their employers by fear and poverty; once they're grown they have nothing: no skills to rely on so the bondage continues.

Among the worst culprits here are the match and fireworks industries in Sivakasi, the bangle and glass factories in Faizabad, food and tea stalls, carpet makers...to name only a few. And, as with everything else, girls are worse off than boys. They're more vulnerable to sexual exploitation by their employers and often their peers; domestic work and child rearing, which is what many of them have to do even as children, do not count as child labour in the eyes of the law.

Pro-labour enthusiasts often hold up the caste system in India as a good example of the positive side of child labour. If all child labour is banned, they say, how will the children of carpenters, of ironsmiths, cobblers, learn their fathers' professions? Their opponents argue for a solution that postpones training in the family profession until a later age, after school, say, at around 14 years old, and with the skills passed equally to girls and boys. Without skills, girls are doomed to the endless cycle of remaining forever the wife of a potter, a cobbler's daughter and so on.

Many groups in India have challenged the Child Labour Act, in particular the government's stress on informal education as a solution to the problem. An NGO in Andhra Pradesh, the MV Foundation, is trying out a different strategy — and with some success. It lists child labourers, and persuades employers, or parents, to let them borrow the children for a day. The children are then taken on a picnic, while volunteers for the group observe the adults who are left behind to see how they cope with the chores that were allotted to the children. Slowly, the amount of time for which the children are taken away is increased, and gradually a process of dialogue to convince them of the importance of education begins. Interestingly, the group has found that boys often run away. The girls, however, assert their wish for an education: they want to learn. One of the children they've managed to put into school so far has returned to work. But according to Professor Shanta Sinha of the MV Foundation, the mere fact of going to school is in itself an education.

More such imaginative strategies and solutions are what is needed. As part of their campaign against child labour, and their questioning of the law, anti-child-labour activists plan a public hearing on child labour later this year. 'We expect children from all over the country to come and speak,' they say. 'Perhaps that, if nothing else, will shock people into some kind of awareness.' ❏

*Urvashi Butalia is a founder of the publishing house Kali for Women, Delhi*

# BABEL

WORLD IN ACTION

*On the streets of Istanbul 1996: police brutality is commonplace*

# The young Turks

ACCORDING to Amnesty International's November 1996 report, *Turkey: Children at Risk of Torture, Death in Custody and 'Disappearance'*, the torture and abuse of children in Turkish prisons is increasing. 'Children as young as 12, sometimes arrested on suspicion of minor charges, are treated with appalling cruelty,' says the report, citing the case of Döne Talun (see below). Children, it claims, 'have become the latest target of both sides in the long-running war opposing government and army to the Kurdish Workers' Party (PKK). Turkish and Kurdish adolescents have been arrested and tortured following spurious allegations of 'belonging to a terrorist organisation'; others have 'disappeared' and died in police custody with little or no attempt to bring the offending officers to justice.

Turkey, which ratified the UN Convention on the Rights of the Child in 1995, vigorously denies AI's accusations along with the latter's claim that the government 'has done nothing at all to put an end to the violence'. But AI's allegations are confirmed by Onder Ozcalipci, a member of the Human Rights Medical Foundation set up 10 years ago to deal with victims of state violence. Dr Ozcalipci says: 'Reported torture cases are on the increase. Though most of those tortured are adult, at least 60 children were tortured by the Turkish police force last year, more than twice the number of the previous year.' He adds: 'Torture is systematic in our country. Our foundation publishes an annual report recording the evidence we have gathered.'

WORLD IN ACTION

**Abdullah Salman** *lives in Istanbul. By the age of 13, he was working in a shop. One day his employers said some money was missing and along with three older men he was brought to the local police station and held overnight. After three days in police custody Abdullah was released. No charges were brought against him.*

'They said: "We'll give you time. Write down on a paper who took this money." They let everybody write something on paper. That didn't work. So they called the police. There were six or seven people [at the police station]. They blindfolded me. They took me inside. They made me lie down. It was a wet floor.

'I was blindfolded but I felt them put something on my toes. I couldn't see but I'm sure it was something round. He gave me the electric shock and the pain came through my leg. It was so bad I thought I was going to die. I couldn't feel my legs. I screamed. I was crying and telling them that I wouldn't say that I had done it just because they were hurting me. But they carried on with the torture.'

**Sayzie Salman** [his mother]: 'I tried to hug him but he pulled himself away from me. He backed off in a way. He was filthy and smelled of urine. I hardly stopped myself from crying. He was unrecognisable. He was covered in bruises. There were also bloodstains on his face and neck. There was no part of his body which was not bruised. I went back to the investigation bureau to ask why they had done this.'

*An independent doctor examined Abdullah and confirmed that he'd been tortured. Mrs Salman complained to the public prosecutor. An officer was prosecuted, given a three-month suspended prison sentence and is now back at work.*

**Mahir Goktas** *of Izmir is 14. Last December [1995], along with 16 other teenagers, he was picked up by the police who said he was a member of an illegal political organisation. Mahir was held by the Anti-Terror Police under the Anti-Terrorist law.*

'First they undressed me and took me to a cold shower. I was given a cold shower in the toilet. Then we went back to the room and they started giving me electric shocks. They connected wires to my right toe and then they gave me electric shock through my testicles. They also gave me electric shocks on my chest and arms. This lasted about 15 or 20 minutes. I nearly passed out and they poured cold water on me. They said we're pouring bleach on you and you will die. They wanted me to admit to some crimes. They used to gather around and decide who to blame for what. They decided to accuse me of putting up posters and throwing molotov cocktails. They used to write down the statements themselves and ask us to sign it. I don't remember making any statements at the police station. I just signed the statements they had prepared.'

*The children's parents were refused access to the prison so asked a local MP, Sabri Ergul to intervene. Inside the police station, he heard a scream:*

**Sabri Ergul**: 'I went to the room where the screams were coming from and opened the door. When I went inside the room I saw one of the girls lying fully naked on the floor. She was blindfolded. One of the children was standing up and the other boy, whom I knew, was sitting down. There was also another boy standing up. I was shocked with what I had seen. There were five or six police officers around the girl on the floor and there was a device on the table which I think was used for giving electric shocks. I wasn't expecting to see such a thing so I just stood there shocked. I got hold of the children's medical reports. The children had passed out during electric shock treatment; they'd had truncheons inserted into their anus; the girls had been sexually harassed and they'd been taken to hospital. But the police had hidden these things from the files. I went to the hospital and collected all the documents one by one.

I wrote up what I saw and publicised it. I gave the file to the prime minister and hung a notice saying 'Torture exists in Turkey' outside her office. But she [Tansu Ciller] didn't show any interest.'

*After interrogation it was claimed that the children confessed. They were put on trial, but their MP collected evidence that led to another trial, this time of 10 police officers accused of torturing the schoolchildren.*

WORLD IN ACTION

**Döne Talun** *lives with her family in the slums of Ankara, an area seldom visited by tourists. She was 13 years old when she got into trouble with the police. The local police held her for a day then handed her over to a special police unit who brought her to Ankara police headquarters. The police wanted her to confess to stealing a wallet. They took her to a small room and attached her hands to a machine:*

'I had gone to visit my aunt in Cubuk. I was hungry and didn't have any money on me. I helped myself to a breadcake from one of the stands but the seller hit me and I ran away. They caught me and took me to the police... Whenever he turned that machine on my eyes felt like they were going to pop out of their sockets. I had my blindfold removed and I saw him in front of me. There were others as well. He stopped giving me electric shocks and started hitting me on the back. He also hit me on the head with a walkie-talkie. This part of my head was fractured when I came home. My eyes felt like they were going to pop out of their sockets and I was screaming but they didn't stop. They were telling me to shut up and kicking my back.

'He then went back to the electric thing and turned it on again.

'I asked what wallet was he talking about but he started to turn that thing again. Then they threw me in the other room. One day passed and they started hitting me again. They touched my face a bit with the electric. I still have an electric mark on my face here. He then said to me if I was a woman they would have given electric shocks to my other parts, so I should be grateful for being a girl.'

**Ender Buyukculha** [member of family]: 'We were seriously concerned when we were told of Döne's arrest. Because despite all our attempts the police denied having her under custody and held her for more than 24 hours. After Döne was released, we witnessed torture marks on her body. This evidence of torture was documented by the Human Rights Association and by the medical institution run by the Ministry of Justice.

'The prosecutors' report, which is based on existing medical evidence, neither confirms nor denies that torture took place. In that sense, the torture is accepted. But the report says the torture wasn't applied by those policemen mentioned in the investigation. This means that the state accepts the torture but cannot identify the officers responsible or take them to court.

*Döne's family complained to the public prosecutors about her ordeal. After a year the prosecutors decided not to take action against the police.*

**Cemile Talun** [Döne's mother]: 'They shouldn't do these things to a little girl. If she's done wrong there are courts and prosecutors in this country; they should punish her if necessary. She shouldn't have been beaten for doing nothing; she's only a little girl.'

*In a Turkish cemetery a father tends an unmarked grave. He thinks it contains the body of his 14-year-old son but he can't be sure.* **Cetin Karakoyun** *was picked up by Mersin police in connection with the theft of a TV set. One day later the police sent for his father, Imam Karakoyun. They said Cetin had fallen from a balcony and brought Imam to this grave.*

'The police chief took my arm and we walked up and down in the street. He said I'm very sorry, sir. There's been an accident and your son is dead. I said for God's sake, Mr Police Chief, how did he die? How did this happen? What are you saying? Where is my son? Show me. He said, here,

here. He said we've collected some money for you. We'll give it to you. Don't let anybody know. You don't see us. We don't see you.'

*Imam was suspicious and contacted the local human rights association. They obtained the official post-mortem for his son. It showed that Cetin had been badly beaten and then shot in the head. The police explained that one of their officers had been cleaning his gun when it had accidentally gone off, killing Cetin.*

'I don't know what to think. There is law. There is justice. If he had stolen something or done anything wrong, they should have put him in prison. Why would they need to kill him? Why do they torture and kill a 14-year-old boy? Why did they kill him? It was not an accident, they killed him intentionally.'

*The police officer who shot Cetin Karakoyun was arrested and charged with involuntary manslaughter. He was kept in custody for three months and then released. He was not suspended from duty and is currently on active duty.*

*Much of what happens inside Turkish police stations is secret. But* **Nurhan Varli**, *the daughter of a policeman, the wife of another and herself for 23 years a member of the force, describes the torture rooms used by the police:*

'I saw one such room in a different department across from where I worked. They are all covered with soundproofing material so that screams of the people cannot be heard from the outside. There are some rings on the walls and other torture equipment such as wooden sticks used for beating the soles of the feet. There were also electric shock machines which can be easily transported if required. That's what I saw.

'To make someone confess, physical and psychological pressures are applied. Let's say, for example, preventing the suspect from sleeping, making him stand on one leg, making him eat salt, starving the suspect of food and water, beating the suspect and giving electric shocks with a special machine.' ❏

*Excerpted from* The Young Turks, *a TV documentary from World in Action, made for Granada Television and broadcast in the UK in November 1996. For further information on Turkey see the World in Action website: http://www. granadatv.co.uk/worldinaction*

# DIARY

## MILENA MAHON

# Balkan borders

Geographic Macedonia

I GREW up in the Balkans during the Cold War when the location of my homeland was defined by the battle of ideologies. Bulgaria was supposedly closer to Russia and the German Democratic Republic than to Greece or Yugoslavia. Geography was a political concept. Those territories that were permitted to us were generally beyond reach; the neighbouring territories beyond possibility.

Now, despite wars and other devastations, the Balkans (except for Bosnia) are more open and I could visit parts of my home region for the first time. I travelled easily and safely and found Balkan multiculturalism alive and enticing. But, by the end of my short tour, I was also confused: which were external and which internal borders; which geographical and which political; which ethnic and which linguistic?

The more I struggled to articulate such distinctions, the more definitions escaped me. They were slippery and elusive, refused to stay in place; uncertain and fearful too. In Macedonia, which is struggling to forge its own identity, a Bulgarian does not need a dictionary to communicate. In the Serbian province of Kosovo, Albanians predominate, but only Serbs are bank clerks. In Vojvodina, one can get by with Hungarian or German (and learn that Andy Warhol was Ruthenian). Albania was a place to practise my old Russian, a reminder of a brief mutual connection in the past. Through such shifts and changes, the borders I crossed sat uncomfortably on people's lives and hurt them like a new pair of shoes.

## BORDER: BULGARIA/MACEDONIA

M Y trip begins from my old home, Sofia. Balkan internationalism is most alive in the bus stations, where one hears all languages at once and written destinations never quite explain people's routes. Why is an Albanian woman going to Thessaloniki from Sofia, and where is her last stop? She hardly looks like a tourist. An older man I take to be her father gives her a parting hug, then asks me the time, in perfect Bulgarian. Each trip is an expedition in Balkan history.

I board the bus to Skopje. It is early morning, but the sun already promises a searing day. A packed breakfast is included: a bottle of insipid lemonade and a waffle — courtesy, no doubt, of the new market reforms. Occasionally the bus stops in a village, where somebody gives the driver a spare car part, a sack of flour, a bag with presents, all to be delivered over the border.

The border we are approaching was closed not only because of Yugoslavia's split with the Soviet Union in 1948 but also because of the 'Macedonian question'. Bulgaria has historically denied the existence of a Macedonian nation; Bulgarian Communism addressed this problem by sealing the border with its supposed national brothers.

Sofia still rejects the Macedonian nation but, since the changes, it has recognised the Macedonian state. And the borders are open. The long winter lines of petrol trucks from the days of the Greek embargo have passed, and the Macedonian officer asks Bulgarians and other foreign citizens to produce 50DM, a cheap entry guarantee compared to the funds western embassies demand to see from their visa applications.

Passengers from a 'third country', usually Albanians, are asked more searching questions, as are the Roma (Gypsies), whose citizenship seems not to count. The middle-aged man sitting next to me is from Albania and speaks some Macedonian. But he cannot write it and while we wait in the slow queue, he asks me to fill in his entry papers while he joins the smokers outside. One Gypsy woman, tearful, cannot show the necessary cash and is turned back. 'Why didn't you tell me? I could have lent you money,' the bus driver reprimands. She will come another day. A

*Skopje, Macedonia 1996: Albanian children with their school certificates*

Bulgarian woman complains about the tedious waiting: 'All this to show us that they also have power now. It is the inferiority complex of Macedonia!' Old habits die hard, but it is too hot and nobody is interested in talking politics.

### BORDER: MACEDONIANS/ALBANIANS

AFTER a worrying moment lost in the bus station's diffuse 'arrivals' section, I am picked up by my friend Kim and find that my stay in Macedonia will, after a fashion, be brief. Kim has some renown as a writer working in three languages, Albanian, Macedonian and Serbian. But I am to stay exclusively with him and his family in the suburban Albanian village of Saraj. As the car deviates from the main route to the unpaved side roads, he extends his arm and pronounces: 'From this point on everyone knows you are my guest and you are absolutely safe any time of day or night — at least for now.'

Old men are sitting and talking; children play here and there; women are not to be seen outside the walls of the housing compounds. Classic Ottoman-style houses are surrounded by walls, and the newer have still higher, spectacular whitewashed walls, like fortresses. In the 1980s, Kim explains, the Yugoslav Macedonian authorities decided that the Albanians were hiding behind these walls plotting, and tore many of them down. In consequence, the present perimeters seem built to make a point. 'Too high for a Macedonian bird to fly over,' I venture. My companions — several households of Kim's extended family live within — are cautious, but can't repress a triumphant laugh. The little babies in the communal yard start crying when I speak to their mothers in Macedonian because they think I am a doctor. No other Macedonian speakers ever visit.

That evening a couple of men sit in a little coffee shop and heatedly discuss the sudden news that Ibrahim Rugova, the Albanian leader from Kosovo, has died. No-one else has heard this, but one man insists it was on the radio. The evening is so dull and still it seems improbable that anything at all could happen. By the morning we learn the truth: it was Andreas Papandreou, the Greek leader, who died. Greece may be causing problems for Macedonia but for an Albanian here, it is hardly important. Everyone's mind is preoccupied with their own worries. Rumours at least travel freely across the Balkan borders.

## BORDER: MACEDONIA/ALBANIA

I TAKE a day trip to Podgradetz, a town over the border in Albania. My Albanian guide is a young student in economics in Skopje who sings in a restaurant to support his family. En route, he explains that he will switch to the outlawed Albanian university in Tetovo because the head of the Skopje University once asked him to change his Albanian name to a Macedonian one. 'I have always been a good Muslim,' he boasts. But he lets on that his favourite summer drink is vodka with lemon.

On the way we stop at the famous St Naum Orthodox monastery on Lake Ohrid, one of the most beautiful places in the Balkans. To the south, very, very near, is Albania. It is as if this symbol of Macedonian nationhood had been placed thus to sharpen the demarcation line.

The border itself is bare and desolate, like a desert, with slow, dull armed guards out of an American western. When I fill out an entry form, one asks if he can have my pen. Enver Hoxha's paranoid concrete bunkers are everywhere.

Podgradetz has 25,000 inhabitants, and claims to have had a more peaceable past than many other Balkan settlements. A small percentage of the population are Macedonian and Greek; Bulgarian nationalists claim that some are 'original Bulgarians' from Ottoman times, but I find no-one I can call a compatriot.

These days Podgradetz has a market where pieces of meat are sold in the open air in temperatures well above 35°C. Brick houses are unplastered and people have faces darkened by hard lives. It feels so poor and out of time I do not dare to take out my camera. But two women who serve us in their own coffee shop are very friendly. They have visited their Albanian 'brethren' in Macedonia, but prefer Albania because here it is accepted that women work.

## BORDER: MACEDONIA/SERBIA

ANOTHER dusty bus takes me from Skopje to Pristina, the capital of the Serbian region of Kosovo, previously an autonomous Yugoslav province and now under Serbian military control. Here, in the 'cradle of Serbness', police checks are endless. The long waiting on heated roads and the feeling of vulnerability when asked rudely to open luggage reminds me of television pictures from the Bosnian war and bus routes with sinister destinations. An elderly man with a thick shabby winter jacket makes me especially nervous. He stands mute in the queue for 'Yugoslav passport holders', with a firm grip on a see-through plastic bag full of my favourite, the long light-green peppers. I fear for him. And why on earth does he have to carry these peppers — another Balkan peasant on the move, they make him look even more helpless. Besides, why would he bother: every Balkan household has plenty of peppers!

Finally Pristina surfaces in a dry, colourless valley. The centre of the city is dense with young Albanians drinking coffee under the shelters amid the blasting sound of the latest international Top Twenty, while Serbian police patrol among the tables. There is almost no work for Albanians so they have little else to do.

Albanian politicians' headquarters face the county gaol, the university and the hospital are deserted, Serbian refugees live in gloomy concrete blocks. Even the tranquillity of the Albanian houses is only a superficial relief. 'We hardly know anything about our Serbian neighbours, just that they don't take off their shoes at home,' one young woman explains. 'But nor do we know what future awaits our children.'

The pressure of life in Kosovo doesn't mean, however, that residents are any less attached to their own place. My host Aferdita, wife of a journalist who is studying English literature in the Albanians' parallel or underground school system, has just received an invitation for an exhibition of an Albanian artist from Tirana. 'But I am not from Albania,' she says. 'I'm an Albanian from Kosovo and here is my only home.'

On another day trip we again skirt the Albanian border. I have only read about Prizren and its legendary mystic cults and magic places. It is an hour and a half from Pristina by bus, still within Kosovo, but I take my passport along anyway. From the hills, its narrow, cobbled streets and spreading red roofs look something like Florence, but with the addition of rising minarets and the tall spires of old Orthodox churches. Adding to the mix, many Albanians here speak Turkish, too.

Our friends see us off with wishes that next time they will host us in a free and independent Kosovo. Their small child chants, 'Berisha, Berisha!' (the Albanian president). I am confused about the Albania-Kosovo relationship. Leaving behind these Balkan houses, rightly known for their generous hospitality, makes me sick at heart. Nobody knows how long their children will be allowed to grow up in peace.

Finally to Prevalatz, high in the mountains, the last stop before Albania. There is no checkpoint here and the landscape is desolate. Now and then a bareback rider passes slowly and triumphantly. One hears only the bells of the goats grazing undisturbed on the hills. The politics of Kosovo seem far away.

## BORDER: KOSOVO/SERBIA

I TAKE the dull bus ride to the capital of Serbia with expectation. Belgrade once represented liberal Yugoslav socialism and served as a regional cultural centre. On arrival, it reminds me only of pre-1989 Sofia.

At the too appropriately named Hotel Mosckva, over a solitary coffee

*Prizren, Kosovo 1996: Florence with minarets*

and the familiar Cyrillic script of the Serbian papers, I remember our young hopes as Bulgarian literature students when we longed to mix with the Belgrade milieu. (Paris was beyond dreaming.) Oh well, perhaps it was only our imaginations that were poor, I conclude, as I pay my bill. But is that tall man with the sunglasses following me, or is this, too, my imagination?

Belgrade looks tattered and disappointed but still stands beautifully on the river and comes alive during the long summer nights. Students are on the streets everywhere, as if they own the place — indeed, as they will be with much more determination some months after my visit. Walking down the central Knez Mihaila Street, my new friend Gordana says, 'Something was broken in me and my city. But still, I do not fear the future.'

## BORDER: SERBIA/VOJVODINA

THE train to Novi Sad, the regional capital of the other former autonomous province of Serbia, Vojvodina. As though to confirm the belief that Balkan geography signals cultural changes too, Vojvodina is

*Kosovo, Serbia: Albanians on the move, always under the eye of the Serbian military*
*Credit: Melanie Friend/Panos Pictures*

surprisingly clean and comfortable. This same train continues to the Hungarian border, but I am told that at the point where the river Sava flows into the Danube (near the Vojvodina line), I have already crossed the real border between the Balkans and central eastern Europe.

Vojvodina is an authentic remnant of the Habsburg empire. People representing 23 nationalities live here. There are Catholic, Eastern Orthodox and Uniat (Greek/Catholic) churches. The university has a Ruthenian faculty of culture. Appropriately, my guide is an ethnographer who explains to me how the ethnic map has changed, with the departure of Hungarians and the arrival recently of Serb refugees from Croatia and Bosnia. 'The newcomers are building in Dalmatian style and listen to different music,' he says. The concert hall, he notes, used to be a synagogue.

My friend Sarita introduces me to her landlady, Sophie, a woman of Jewish, German and Hungarian background who married a Serb. 'I brought up my children to be all these, but now I ask myself if it wouldn't have been better to give them just one clear identity. I don't know whether I was misled or if the world has changed.'

Another friend comes and brings *baklava* from Sarajevo where his wife and three children are refugees. Nusret is a Bosnian Muslim from Srebrenica who escaped to Novi Sad during the war. The rest of his family disappeared, and he hopes to trace them through Amnesty International. 'The politicians did it all. We will have to live together again, where else could we go?' he says sorrowfully, but without bitterness.

The border separating this kind of experience may be the biggest one I have faced so far. 'I can check for you in London,' I offer hesitantly, aware, my mind turning towards departure from my old homelands, that I am at the same time also a foreigner. Perhaps I, too, am making just one more promise to the Balkans that will not be kept. ❏

*Milena Mahon is a producer at the BBC World Service Bulgarian section*

# LEGAL

*http://www.McSpotlight.org, London 1996: co-Defendants Helen Steel and Dave Morris*

### D D GUTTENPLAN

# McPrisoners of conscience

**McDonald's took London Greenpeace to court for libel. It's already the longest running trial in British history and by the time the expected judgement in favour of McDonald's is given, will have brought Britain's archaic and draconian libel laws into serious disrepute**

HERE'S something to bear in mind the next time you see the Golden Arches: from February 1986 to October 1990 the McDonald's Corporation threatened to take at least 45 different British groups to court for saying uncomplimentary things about their burgers. The objects of these threats ranged from major news organisations like Granada Television, the *Daily Mail* and the BBC to the Bromley and Hayes *News Shopper*, the *Nuneaton and Bedworth Trader* and the *Leeds Student Magazine*. In every case the threats worked: retractions were issued, apologies offered, material withheld from broadcast or publication.

Then, in September 1990, the American fast food giant issued libel writs against five members of London Greenpeace — a tiny anarchist groupuscule with no connection to Greenpeace International. Facing the prospect of a potentially ruinous trial and, like all libel defendants in Britain, denied legal aid, the five were advised to settle. Given that it can cost £100,000 in legal fees before a case even gets to court, with barristers, junior barristers, solicitors and clerks adding thousands of pounds a day once a trial starts, this was realistic advice. 'There is no other area of the law where the defendant is so much at the mercy of the plaintiff's wealth,' says Geoffrey Robertson QC.

Three members of London Greenpeace did settle. But Helen Steel, a former gardener from Yorkshire, and Dave Morris, a redundant London postal worker, decided to fight. Though Morris and Steel denied either writing or distributing 'What's wrong with McDonald's?', a six-page broadside criticising the company's record on health, the environment, animal rights and labour relations, they said that they agreed with the contents and would defend them in court if necessary.

In pre-trial hearings McDonald's argued that the issues involved were too complicated for a jury to understand. Besides, said Richard Rampton QC, a jury trial might take as long as six or seven weeks, as opposed to 'three to four weeks for judge alone...more likely three than four, I would guess.' Mr Justice Rodger Bell agreed, and in June 1994, after losing an appeal on legal aid at the European Court of Human Rights, the trial began, with Morris and Steel defending themselves. By the time they had finished, in December 1996, *McDonald's v Morris and Steel* had entered the record books as the longest-running trial in British history.

In its early stages the case attracted little notice among either the press or human rights organisations. As the trial wore on, however, the David versus Goliath nature of the contest, and the record-setting length of the proceedings, began to attract media attention. This was bad news for McDonald's, whose actions throughout the trial have made it look remarkably like the greedy, bullying corporate behemoth (hiding behind the grinning rictus of Ronald McDonald) depicted on the cover of 'What's wrong with McDonald's?'

Worse yet, in February 1995, after months of unsavoury revelations about the company's practices — including the news that McDonald's hired two separate firms of private detectives to infiltrate the dozen or so members of London Greenpeace — supporters of Morris and Steel launched McSpotlight, a World Wide Web site devoted to 'McDonald's, McLibel, Multinationals'. Based in Holland (beyond the reach of British law), McSpotlight links 100 megabytes of material including the banned 'What's wrong with McDonald's' (available in 14 languages), a complete, indexed transcript of the trial, an order form for McLibel T-shirts and badges, and nearly every film clip, cartoon, or article McDonald's has ever tried to suppress — not to mention promos for *McLibel: Burger Culture on Trial,* Morris and Steel's book on the case, coming soon from Macmillan to a bookshop near you.

Or maybe not so soon. Neil Hamilton MP recently managed to persuade a number of British booksellers not to stock *Sleaze: The Corruption of Parliament,* two *Guardian* reporters' account of the parliamentary cash-for-questions scandal, simply by threatening to issue writs. 'This is something [Sir James] Goldsmith started and [Robert] Maxwell took up,' said *Guardian* editor Alan Rusbridger. 'Threatening to sue booksellers and distributors is quite a potent weapon.'

The judge's decision in McLibel is not expected before the end of March, but Dave Morris is realistic about his chances: 'Most of the judgement will be bad news for McDonald's, but that's going to be in the small print.' That the headlines would proclaim victory for McDonald's was practically a foregone conclusion — if not from the moment the writs were served, certainly from the moment Morris and Steel were denied a jury trial. 'The judge didn't even include our case in his summing up,' said Alan Rusbridger just days after the *Guardian* won a suit brought by the Police Federation. 'We'd have lost without a jury.'

If Morris and Steel do lose, they will be held liable for McDonald's legal costs. The company, despite frequent public statements to the contrary, has also asked for £100,000 in damages. Given the defendants' combined income of £7,500 a year, 'we could have an amount deducted from our pay cheques, or our income support, for years,' said Helen Steel. McDonald's has also sought an injunction barring Morris or Steel from repeating any of the criticisms made in the leaflet. Defy that, says Steel, and 'we could go to jail.'

Loss of income, suppression of free speech, potential loss of liberty: McLibel, says barrister Keir Starmer, is 'an enormously important human rights issue. It brings the whole of British libel law into question.'

Not all human rights campaigners agree. Lord Lester (whose arguments in *Derbyshire County Council v Times Newspapers* recently established that, in the interests of robust scrutiny, governmental bodies are not allowed to

• • • • • • • • • • • • • • • • • • • • • • • • • • • • • • • • •

**Loss of income, suppression of free speech, potential loss of liberty: McLibel is an enormously important human rights issue. It brings the whole of British libel law into question**

• • • • • • • • • • • • • • • • • • • • • • • • • • • • • • • • •

sue their critics for libel) didn't 'know enough about the issues to comment'. John Wadham, director of the civil rights organisation Liberty (which helped Morris and Steel in their appeal for legal aid) felt that the denial of legal aid in libel cases was the main problem, and wanted funds made available to both potential plaintiffs and defendants. When it was suggested this might result in an even greater 'chilling effect' on the press, Wadham replied: 'If newspapers get it wrong, they should pay.'

Wadham had little patience for the suggestion that what Britain needed was an American-style First Amendment to protect free speech. 'The First Amendment gets it wrong,' he said, 'Article 19 [of the Universal Declaration of Human Rights] gets it right.' Yet it should perhaps be noted that only in Britain, a signatory to both the Universal Declaration of Human Rights and the similarly worded European Convention on Human Rights, can a US corporation use the courts to muzzle its critics. And McDonald's is not the only American venue-shopper. The drug company Upjohn, for example, recently won a £25,000 judgment against a Scottish doctor for a statement reported in *The New York Times* — a paper whose UK circulation, though negligible, was apparently sufficient for the British courts to claim jurisdiction.

American companies seldom bother to bring such claims into US courts for the simple reason that they would lose. Under US law the burden of proof in a libel action is on the plaintiff, who must prove they have been falsely defamed, rather than on the defendant. And since the Supreme Court ruling in *New York Times v Sullivan* in 1964, any plaintiff who qualifies as a 'public figure' — a category broad enough to include McDonald's, members of the Royal Family and most government officials — has to prove the offending statements were made in malicious or reckless disregard of the truth.

Nor are British corporations reluctant to use the libel laws to discourage scrutiny. Eric Barendt, Goodman professor of media law at University College, London, named British Nuclear Fuels as one of several UK companies with litigious reputations. The number of suits which go to trial is quite small, said Professor Barendt. But as Justin Walford, the in-house lawyer for Express Newspapers, points out, in most cases a telephone call, a letter, or a writ is sufficient. 'Maxwell didn't actually sue all that often,' he said. In the long run, says Walford, McDonald's costs in McLibel may be a sound investment. 'Anyone else tempted to criticise them on similar grounds will know they are dealing with a company prepared to spend six years and £10 million. Would you risk it?'

If the Labour Party win the next election, they have promised to incorporate the European Convention on Human Rights into British law. It would then be up to British judges to decide how to apply Article 10 guaranteeing freedom of expression. The problem, says Alan Rusbridger, is that 'English judges are very cautious about expanding the law of qualified privilege' to create a kind of 'public figure' category. Martin Soames, a solicitor who often works on libel cases, suggests that Parliament might agree to creating such an exemption as 'a quid pro quo for a privacy law'. Geoffrey Robertson is sceptical: 'You won't get any sense out of Parliament because it's politicians who make the most money out of libel.'

If neither the courts nor Parliament are prepared to act, is free speech to remain forever at the mercy of corporate predators? Perhaps not. Andrew Clapham, an attorney with Amnesty International, points out that international law is beginning to grapple with what he calls 'the privatisation of human rights'. While we usually think of human rights as being restrictions on state action, says Clapham, 'the effect is the same whether you're being strip-searched by the state or by a private security company.'

Clapham argues that the use of libel laws to suppress dissent — even if the dissent is over the links between diet and health — is already a violation of international law. Clapham points to *The Sunday Times* case when the European Court of Human Rights, in finding that the newspaper had a right to publish material relating to the effects of the drug Thalidomide despite a court order not to do so, effectively overruled a House of Lords decision affirming the British contempt of court law.

Could the same thing happen in McLibel? Keir Starmer thinks it should. Starmer, who says he will represent Morris and Steel if they appeal to Strasbourg, says the current law is absurd. 'If I run you down in the road and break your legs, I'm only liable for damages if I failed to exercise reasonable care. Our libel laws place a higher value on reputation than on personal security or indeed life itself.'

If the libel law is overturned, those politicians charged with drafting a replacement might want to consider the more vigorous protections for free speech recently enacted in New York and California. There, too, corporations — particularly property developers and logging companies — have used libel to intimidate critics. Though the suits were seldom successful, getting dragged into court was both costly and time-consuming. In order to combat the chilling effects of what are known in the US as SLAPP (Strategic Lawsuits Against Public Participation), legislators in both states passed laws protecting potential defendants who, in the words of the California statute, exercise their 'right of petition or free speech...in connection with a public issue'.

'It doesn't stop them from being sued,' says Victor Kovner, a First Amendment specialist in New York. 'But it allows a judge to dismiss a case very early, and provides for recovery of costs' and, in some cases, punitive damages. The basic issue, says Andrew Clapham, 'is how to get, say, Robert Maxwell, to be held liable for violating your freedom of expression.' For Morris and Steel, no change in the law will give them back the two years spent in Mr Justice Bell's courtroom. But then, no decision of a British court will be able to silence McSpotlight. ❏

*D  D Guttenplan worked as a newspaper reporter, columnist and media critic in New York and now lives in London, where he is writing a biography of I F Stone*

# LITERATURE

## GHAZI RABIHAVI

# David

A PERSON would have to be stupid, stupid for a person to, Your
Excellency, I'm feeling dizzy, you're absolutely right with your eyes
shut and your head reclining gently against the headrest, it being my
duty to report to you I have to say there's nothing happening even the
writers. I have discovered one doesn't smoke one's pipe in this humble
servant's room otherwise one does smoke a pipe I know this and only
this I know time permitting you could read some of their written
writings but you can't, having time doesn't agree with Your Excellency's
disposition Your Excellency even with your eyes shut. My task is to read
look listen and to protect art's boundaries of course until further notice
we have also banned its cococonsumption, as you say they do not pay
attention the main point is battle not forbearance, forbearance? One
moment please, the dictionary is right here patient self-control,

tolerance. Towards whom? Towards the attackers of our noble culture, I thought you were singing under your breath I'm sorry as Your Excellency quite rightly said we have so many tales in our culture I told them to write the old story about Mullah Nasreddin and his mule rewrite it so that the people could enjoy it they like that sort of thing battle against innovation and civilisation. Rest assured they're banned, as long as they ignore our mission pay no attention to the past, now that our very existence lies in the past, long live the past the past, today one buries the present like the future under mountains of soil soil like women's hair, I'm sorry. One of the writers has described a scene on a bus where the men sit with their backs to the women there are two seats in front of the women facing one another, I suggest we write a circular to the municipality so that they can officially order the bus company to eliminate the two seats. Have they ever stopped and considered whom these nudge-nudge-wink-winks will ultimately benefit? See, sin. What was that sound it bothers my ear now and then I say this from the bottom of my heart I feel like seeing scenes of war war again in the streets in the alleys along with its rhythms of mourning, I wish I'd told them that this humble servant is himself a student of philosophy I said A humanist artist tends to write about the most despicable and depraved aspects of human affairs, the painter and the sculptor display the naked human figure the height of artistic depravity, David's statue the height of human depravity, how fortunate for Your Excellency not to have to carry the sin of having seen it or seeing it in the future quite right Sir there's no point in arguing with them but to be honest I would once again demonstrate my capabilities and loyalty among my colleagues otherwise what ought not to be seen heard read by the people will be confined to the deep office dustbin by your humble servant under Your Excellency's supervision of course in a deep deep dustbin, dark, rest assured forget about a lantern not even a thousand searchlights would reveal that which is in the depths — don't worry please remain in your reclining position, it is only the dogs who sniff through the garbage for a crust of bread and the beggars for a rag to cover up their naked chests from the wind and everyone for a piece of bread and how ignorant they are about the noble labour of art that was depicted in sacrifices and passed away. Nothing must be at the service of abominable humanity we have granted our very all to our sanctities so that our bodies and lives will be encircled with the golden

fortress of morality and our souls ultimately released released released —
as Your Excellency realises I strive endlessly to improve and correct, and
whenever I encounter a delusory phrase that may perturb my mind I
draw a line under it in people's minds. It is my task to draw a red line
under all delusions and ambiguities in which lie the slightest hint of
living wanting freely, how difficult living has become today, Your
Excellency does not have a little girl, but I'm sure you love all little
girls. I would hereby like to put to you the suggestion that we should
ban them before they take their seats in their studies in front of that
white white white so that it is never blackened and does not slither its
way into our realm, so that the people are not smitten with the urge to
know although nothing ought to be said about the nightly prowls
around the office dustbin which is only the work of beggars and dogs, if
we could ban the creation before its creation, we would no longer have
a bin full of writings, paintings, sculptors so that anyone other than
those mentioned might set out awandering lantern in hand. When I
take a deep breath there is a shooting pain in the bone under my heart
especially on winter nights when there blows a bitter wind but not so
strong that it could extinguish the lantern, if only it would, the shooting
pain in the bone under the heart is sometimes accompanied by the
sound of qualms qualms qualms quash, although the difficult breathing
of this humble servant is not from any pipe, but from this pipe. When it
is being lit there is nothing a person can do but stare into the mouth of
the pipe in which there is a piling up of a mass of fire conjuring in the
mind the rush of a mass of lanterns towards our office dustbin, how
deep and dark, rest assured Your Excellency, neither a fire's flame nor
the coppery glow of the moon, nothing, can reveal the naked figure of
David. You appreciate how pleasant the smell of the tobacco is in the
pipe? Please allow me to blow blow in your face I'm so sorry I kept
thinking that the snoring sounds meant that you were awake awake —
are you awake? ❏

*Ghazi Rabihavi is an Iranian writer now living in London. All his fiction is
banned, or impounded with the Ministry of Islamic Guidance in Tehran. 'David'
was written in Tehran in 1993*

*Translated by Nilou Mobasser*
*Illustration by Jeff Fisher*

## LIU ZILI

# Quasimodo

A PICTURE was hanging on the wall in the room. A lump of white ice was bobbing up and down on the blue waves in the black frame. It seemed to be knocking against the smooth glass.

There was a large bed in the room. A man was lying motionless on the bed. He had been ill for ages. A woman was sitting as usual in the rocking-chair. She was playing with a stone in her hand. It had been removed from her husband's abdomen. It was multicoloured and glistening. A chair with a carved back stood opposite the woman's rocking-chair, on the left side of the bed. No-one had ever sat in that chair.

The woman watched her deaf-and-dumb husband. He was at death's door. She had no feelings and no illusions. It would happen sooner or later. She just sat in the dust, day after day, waiting for the dust from another place to settle slowly. If her dignified husband was really to be buried one day amid a grand ceremony, then the Quasimodo in her heart would leave the corpse, cross the hall, kick over the large crooked-necked vase by the inlaid wall panel and sit down decidedly in the chair where no-one had ever sat.

She would often engage in conversation with her husband. She spoke both for her husband and for herself. Usually her first question would be:

'Hey, do you see the monster sitting on that chair?'

'No. I can see the sunlight shining on the seat and on the legs...'

'You really don't see it?'

'How annoying! I think you should move the chair away from me!'

'No! I won't. It can't be moved. I'll see it when it comes.'

Why was she waiting so devoutly for a monster, for a Quasimodo? Hadn't she seen enough of her husband's face contorted by illness, his flesh stolen away as if through lack of affection, and spasms brought on by terror? Her husband's body was currently being crushed to pieces by a new power, and was forming itself into a new indignation, one without form, without structure and without a soul. This image formed a striking contrast with his posture, bearing and intelligence before the illness.

Before the illness, his mind and body were at peace, his physique strong, his bearing elegant and his manner very cautious. He belonged to that class of men who were universally considered to have breeding. He did everything without the slightest error: making love, taking meals, going out, coming home, greeting guests, seeing visitors out, reading, writing, conducting experiments, listening to speeches…there were no exceptions. In short, he conformed to the principle of ice. He melted in the season during which it was proper to melt, and froze in the season during which it was proper to freeze. This brought down upon her an unbearable, ceaseless pressure and terror.

After the operation to remove his gallstones, a colourless crystal was extracted from his body and placed in the palm of her hand. It hadn't left her hand since. This was to be a turning-point for them. Afterwards his principles, regulations, customs and habits slowly became flexible and then disintegrated, until one day at dusk the violent pain in his abdomen suddenly disappeared.

However, the turning-point came too late for her. His present irregular condition was the result of nothing more than his vitality being sapped and his senses being weakened. This irregular form was not the one she had envisaged in her mind's eye. The masculinity and beauty she yearned for were embodied in Quasimodo. When the bells rang out in the snow, Quasimodo made his way over, climbing, like a spring breeze. He stretched out those arms as thick as tree-trunks, and the sense of a river running dry could be gleaned from his panting.

At last he sat on the chair that was neither very large nor very sturdy, blocking the contact between his heart and hers with his ape-like body. When the towering partition curtain fell, loneliness filled the room from all sides. It was as though someone had touched a spider's web that had remained undisturbed for a century. Sorrow and misery permeated the air, which began to moan. At first she was pleasantly surprised by this, then she was frightened, and finally her soul completely left her body. The crystal in her hand dropped to the pale wooden floor with a thud. An extremely weak and muffled echo sounded in the room, just as though it were an omen. She was pinned down by four arms. Her

arms were slowly leaving her body.

Her statue was later placed to the right of the picture frame by her descendants. A large mah-jong table was put where the bed had been. The inlaid wooden panel had been replaced by a fake diamond ornament.

None of this could alter her husband's fate. Time passed chaotically following her departure from this world. His limbs detached themselves from his body after having decomposed. His body evaporated. But his indestructible head floated on the ice.

There was no land anywhere near the floating ice. The clear sea water made a ringing sound against it. A colony of penguins was hopping about clumsily and crying without human feeling. ❏

*Liu Zili is a poet and writer of fiction. He was a contributing member of the* Today *group of writers from its beginnings in the late 1970s. He is now working as a journalist in Beijing.* Today *magazine is banned in China*

*Translated by Desmond Skeel*
*Illustrations by Jeff Fisher*